A
Collector's Guide to
THEATRICAL POSTCARDS

A
Collector's Guide to
THEATRICAL POSTCARDS

Richard Bonynge

Grange
BOOKS

A Collector's Guide to
Theatrical Postcards

First published 1988 by Craftsman House,
a division of the Craftsman's Press Pty. Limited

Copyright © 1988 Richard Bonynge

This edition published 1993 by Grange Books
An imprint of Grange Books Limited
The Grange
Grange Yard
London
SE1 3AG

Produced by The Promotional Reprint Company Ltd. UK

ISBN 1 85627 496 9

Printed and bound in China

CONTENTS

Foreword

Collecting postcards has long fascinated people from many walks of life. The postal card was invented in Austria in 1869 and adopted in Great Britain in 1870 Although illustrated postcards had appeared as early as 1871, photographic and illustrated cards in colour really came into their own with the Paris Exhibition of 1889, and by 1895 the craze for sending and collecting postcards was in full swing.

As tourism increased, along with the development of photographic and colour printing methods in the 1880s, so did the output of postcards. Millions were printed in these early years and in Germany alone, by 1897, there were more than a thousand manufacturers of illustrated cards and more than sixty producing postcard albums for collectors. Illustrated cards were perhaps at their most beautiful around the turn of the century, when they were characterised by the art nouveau style.

Until 1897 it was illegal to write a message on the same side as the address, but thereafter many Edwardian ladies and gentlemen exchanged cards with messages ranging from the inane (which seems to have been the norm) to messages of personal interest, as well as titbits relating to the subject of the card. How interesting it is today to read a contemporary opinion of a favourite actor or actress in a play of the day.

Postcards may be classified in endless ways – for example, comic, military, royalty, commemorative, topographical (the most popular and the most common). Bearing in mind that in 1908 alone 860 million cards were sent through the post, it is obvious that the choice for collectors is abundant. It would therefore seem wiser to specialise if a collection is to have any importance.

For those interested in the theatre of the end of the nineteenth century and the first decades of the present one, there is a wealth of knowledge to be found in these old cards which are fortunately still readily available. Although collecting theatrical subjects was all the rage in the early 1900s, the fad declined for thirty years or so until it was revived in the 1960s. There were always collectors, but from the 'sixties onwards postcards became big business. Many big auction houses hold and even specialise in postcard sales; I have appended a small list of some of the English houses (see page 115).

Postcard fairs are frequently held in the British Isles, throughout the United States, in France, Germany, Switzerland and elsewhere. I have found cards in Spain, Portugal, Italy, Sweden, Holland, Belgium, Australia and South America – in antique shops, junk shops and street markets. All that is needed is a little perseverance and some spare time. As one collects one learns, and the knowledge helps to find better and rarer cards. Of course, specialist dealers can assist in locating a desired card, but a great deal of fun is to be had in searching through assorted bundles at a fair – sometimes finding just what one is after, or conversely, something unexpectedly interesting. This is a hobby for rich and poor, and collecting can take place on many levels.

I began collecting in 1950 when I discovered Portobello Market in London and the booths full of cards along the banks of the Seine in Paris. My first interest was in operatic postcards, but in looking for these I came across many cards dealing with ballet and other facets of the theatre, and I soon found myself immersed in collecting anything even vaguely connected with theatre. And what a way to discover its history! After all, it is no good possessing a card and knowing nothing about it.

I always buy cards that I like from a purely visual point of view and sometimes it is years before I find out anything about them. Well-known personalities are easy to recognise, but many who once had a certain fame are not well documented, and celebrities of the circus, music hall and pantomime are particularly difficult to identify. It is necessary to peruse newspapers and magazines of the period, to search through old programs, and delve in libraries. Even so, some characters prove elusive. But often on the very day when one is not conciously looking for it, a scrap of information will turn up and provide another angle of research. In my researches for this volume I have found much contradictory biographical information, most especially regarding birth dates. I have tried to check facts but sometimes have had to resort to the question mark.

Many people collect postcards purely for investment – even bankers and stockbrokers! However, while I am quite aware of the value of many cards, much more pleasure, I find, is to be had from the pure enjoyment of the search. For this reason I have chosen for this book all types of theatrical cards. Some are easy to find and inexpensive; others are virtually impossible to obtain. Commercial values change constantly – generally upwards – and one country, or even one dealer, will value a card differently from another. In Switzerland for example, beautiful, early and rare Swiss postcards are astronomical in price, while many theatre cards can be found for little. On the other hand, in America and France good theatre cards are expensive nowadays, while the English market remains reasonable. Recently the vogue for autographed cards has pushed prices sky high, and those featuring stars such as Eleonora Duse, Anna Pavlova, Lillie Langtry, Tamara Karsavina, Mata Hari, Sarah Bernhardt, Isadora Duncan, Enrico Caruso, Nellie Melba, Colette (as a music hall artist), Feodor Chaliapin, Loie Fuller, and Vaslav Nijinsky are both desirable and fairly rare. The degree of rarity is important, as is the condition of each card. As an example, the card of Haricléa Darclée (no. 27a) is a valuable one. Her picture appears rarely, and to find her autographed photograph in the role of Tosca which she created is rare indeed. Conversely, cards of Gladys Cooper, Phyllis and Zena Dare, or Marie Studholme are plentiful, but no less desirable in a theatrical collection. These actresses appeared in many plays and musical comedies and it is amusing and informative to collect as many of their roles as one can find, which can be identified (with a little patience) from old copies of *Play Pictorial*. There are still legions of actors and actresses, singers and dancers to be found for less than a pound or dollar. The true value of the card, however, will always lie in the eyes of the collector.

This book is divided into categories, and it is perhaps a good idea to start collecting one category only; however, the avid collector will not stop here but will explore a world which becomes ever more fascinating. Collecting postcards can become a way of life. I hope this book will amuse and assist newcomers absorbed by this fascinating hobby, leading to many happy discoveries.

I list below a few sources for the new collector to investigate, although there are now so many publications dealing with postcards throughout the world that anyone devoid of knowledge can soon acquire it.

I would like to express my thanks to Tessa Trench and Dr Darlene Neuman for assisting me in the research required for the book as well as for their splendid typing from my not easily decipherable scribbles.

Richard Bonynge

THEATRICAL POSTCARDS

Ballet

1a   VASLAV NIJINSKY (b. Kiev, 1888; d. London, 1950) dancing
the Lezginka in Fokine's *Le Festin* (1909)
Publisher: Hermann Leiser, Berlin   Photograph: Bert, Paris

Nijinsky, the most famous of all male dancers, studied at the Imperial Ballet School, St Petersburg, then joined the Maryinsky Theatre where he partnered Pavlova, Kschessinska, Preobajenska and Karsavina. He was the star of Diaghilev's Paris season (1909-12) in *Carnaval*, *Schéhérazade*, *Le Spectre de la Rose*, *Petrushka*, and *Daphnis et Chloé*. He choreographed *L'Après-midi d'un Faune* (1912), *Jeux* and *Le Sacre du Printemps* (1913).

On a South American tour in 1913 he married Hungarian dancer Romala de Pulszky, and thereafter Diaghilev, whose feelings for him were more than friendly, severed all connection with him. By the age of twenty-seven Nijinsky had become insane and spent the rest of his life in and out of clinics, in his lucid periods painting and working on a system of dance notation.

Although his dazzling career lasted only ten years, his extraordinary virtuosity and inventive choreography made an indelible mark on the history of ballet.

1b   ADOLF BOLM (b. St Petersburg, 1884; d. Hollywood, 1951)
as the Chief Warrior in Fokine's *Polovtsian Dances* (?)
Photograph: W. Willinger, Berlin

A graduate of the Imperial Ballet School in St Petersburg, Adolf Bolm joined the Maryinsky Theatre in 1903. He toured European capitals with Pavlova (1907-8) and appeared in the Diaghilev seasons in Paris, thereafter becoming a regular member of Diaghilev's Ballet Russe. During the First World War he formed his own company in New York, the Ballet Intime, and in 1919 his production of *The Birthday of the Infanta* for the Chicago Civic Opera established his reputation as a choreographer. In 1928 he created the first production of Stravinsky's *Apollon Musagète* in Washington.

He made America his home and appeared in Ziegfeld and Schubert revues. He choreographed for the Metropolitan and Chicago opera companies as well as for several movies (*The Mad Genius*, *The Men in Her Life*, *The Life of Cellini*) in Hollywood, where he was revered as a teacher until his death.

As a choreographer he is remembered for creating *Foyer de la Danse*, a pantomimic ballet in one act first produced in Chicago in 1927, with music by Chabrier and inspired by Degas' painting of the same name, and *Iron Foundry*, a ballet in one act, first performed at the Hollywood Bowl in 1932.

1c   STANISLAS IDZIKOWSKY (b. Warsaw, 1894; d. London,
1977) in *La Princesse Enchantée*

Stanislas Idzikowsky began his studies as a child in Warsaw and made his first appearance there in the divertissement, *Ali Baba*. He came to London in 1911 where he studied with Cecchetti and appeared in *The Belle of New York* with the Empire Theatre Ballet.

He joined Pavlova for a while in 1913, and in 1914 became part of Diaghilev's Ballet Russe, remaining with the company until 1929. At first he was given Nijinsky's roles in *Carnaval*, *Le Spectre de la Rose*, and *Petrushka*, in all of which he triumphed. Later he created several major ballets for Massine: *The Good-Humoured Ladies* (1917), *Les Contes Russes* (1917), *La Boutique Fantasque* (1919), *Le Tricorne* (1919) and *Pulcinella* (1920). After leaving Diaghilev he created Ashton's *Les Rendezvous* for the Vic-Wells Ballet in 1933.

Idzikowsky had extraordinary elevation and an altogether phenomenal technique which was especially evident as the Blue Bird in *The Sleeping Beauty*, perhaps his most outstanding role.

1d   MIKHAIL MORDKIN (b. Moscow, 1880; d. New Jersey, 1944)
in *La Bayadère*
Photograph: Sacharov & Orlov, 1916

Educated at the Bolshoi Theatre School, Mikhail Mordkin entered the company in 1899 and later became Ballet Master. He danced in the Diaghilev 1909 Paris Season and toured Europe and America with Anna Pavlova in 1909-10. He formed the all-star Imperial Russian Ballet which toured America in 1911-12 with Geltzer, Lopokova, Idzikowsky and Volinine. In 1912 Mordkin rejoined the Bolshoi and was created its Director in 1917.

Leaving Russia after the Revolution, he settled in the United States in 1924. In 1926 he founded the Mordkin Ballet Company which would in 1939 form the basis of Ballet Theatre. He was much esteemed as a choreographer and teacher.

2a   PIERINA LEGNANI (b. 1863; d. 1923)
                         Publisher: 'Richard', St Petersburg
                         Photograph: Imperial Theatres

Pierina Legnani was prima ballerina at La Scala, Milan, from 1892. She was famous for her thirty-two fouettés which were first seen in *Aladdin* in London in 1892, then in Petipa's *Cinderella* in St Petersburg; these were forever after immortalised in *Swan Lake*, which she created in the revised version of 1895 at the Maryinsky Theatre. The original Bolshoi production of 1877 had been less than a success. Legnani also created *Raymonda* (1898) and *Ruses d'Amour* (1900). She danced her last performance in St Petersburg in 1901.

2b   MAUD ALLAN (b. Canada, 1880; d. Los Angeles, 1950) as
                         Salome
                         Rotary Photographic Series   Postmark: 4 October 1912

Maud Allan participated in the revival of ancient Greek dancing, appearing barefoot – often in sparse white draperies. Her most famous ballet, *The Vision of Salome*, first seen in Vienna in 1903 with music by Marcel Remy, was considered very erotic at the time. She toured the world and wrote *My Life and Dancing* (1908).

2c   TAMARA KARSAVINA (b. St Petersburg, 1885; d. Beaconsfield,
                         1978) as Columbine in *Le Carnaval*
                         Publisher: J. Beagles and Co., London   Photograph: Bassano

Tamara Karsavina made her début at the Maryinsky Theatre in 1902 and danced with the company until 1918. She also danced for Diaghilev from 1909. For Fokine she created *Les Sylphides* (1908), *Cléopâtre* (1909), *Carnaval* and *The Firebird* (1910), *Le Spectre de la Rose* and *Petrushka* (1911) and *Daphnis et Chloé* (1912); for Nijinsky, *Jeux* (1913); and for Massine, *Le Tricorne* (1919) and *Pulcinella* (1920).

    She married a British diplomat and lived in London from 1918, appearing as guest with Diaghilev's Ballet Russe. She was with the Ballet Rambert in 1930-31, and wrote her magnificent autobiography *Theatre Street* in 1930. Karsavina was one of the greatest ballerinas.

2d   ANNA PAVLOVA (b. St Petersburg, 1881; d. The Hague, 1931) as
                         Swanilda in *Coppélia*
                         Publisher: Hermann Leiser, Berlin circa 1910
                         Photograph: Ernst Schneider, Berlin

Anna Pavlova entered the Maryinsky Theatre in 1902; there she danced the great classical roles and created her famous *The Dying Swan* (1907), through which she became a household word worldwide. She danced at the Maryinsky until 1913, also appearing with Diaghilev's company. Thereafter she embarked on never-ending world tours, travelling with her own company to North and South America, South Africa, Australasia and the Far East. Her partners were Mordkin, Novikov, Volinine and Vladimiroff. She was not innovative but her name has become synonymous with ballet and she must be counted as the most famous dancer of all time.

a

MAUD ALLAN.

b

MADAME TAMARA KARSAVINA.
THE CELEBRATED RUSSIAN DANCER.

c

Anna Pawlowa

Verlag HERM. LEISER
Berlin W.15.

6063

d

3a MICHEL FOKINE (b. St Petersburg, 1880; d. New York, 1942)
and VERA FOKINA (b. 1886; d. New York, 1958) in *Le Spectre de
la Rose*
Photograph: Axel Ellassons, Stockholm
Postmark: 6 May 1914, Stockholm

The artists are depicted in *Le Spectre de la Rose* which Fokine choreographed for Diaghilev in 1911. Fokine's place in ballet history is assured by his choreography for *The Dying Swan* (1907), *Le Pavillon d'Armide* (1907), *Les Sylphides* (1908), *The Polovtsian Dances* (1909), *Carnaval* (1910), *Schéhérazade* (1910), *The Firebird* (1910), *Petrushka* (1911), and *Daphnis et Chloé* (1912).

Vera Fokina (nee Antonovna) joined the Maryinsky Theatre after graduating from the Imperial Ballet Academy. She married Michel Fokine in 1905 and created the roles of Chiarina in *Carnaval* and the Princess in *The Firebird* in 1910.

3b ISADORA DUNCAN (b. San Francisco, 1877; d. Nice, 1927)

Isadora Duncan was the tempestuous American dancer who threw off the restraints of classical ballet and danced in loose tunics in a style which purported to be that of the ancient Greek dancers. Her fame in Europe was immense but she was accepted less in her own country. This was largely due to her much publicised affairs with the theatre designer Edward Gordon Craig, Paris Singer (of the sewing machine company) and the Russian poet Essenin; her sympathies with the Russian regime also contributed to this situation. Her death was as extravagant as her life – she was killed while driving in a sports car on the French Riviera, strangled by her long scarf which became entangled in the wheel spokes!

3c LYDIA KYASHT (b. St Petersburg, 1815; d. London, 1959) as
Lise in *La Fille Mal Gardée*
Published in aid of The Red Cross
Photograph: K. Fischer, Moscow-St Petersburg

Lydia Kyasht joined the Maryinsky Theatre in 1902 and in 1908 became prima ballerina at the Empire Theatre in London. She also danced in America and for Diaghilev. This costume shows her in *La Fille Mal Gardée*, a two-act ballet by Petipa and Ivanov with music by Peter Ludwig Hertel, first produced in Berlin in 1864. Today this ballet is generally performed with the original sparkling score by Hérold, which was first heard at the Paris Opéra in 1828.

3d VERA CORALLI (b. Moscow, 1889; d. Vienna, 1972) and
ALEXANDRE VOLININE (b. Moscow, 1882; d. Paris, 1955) in
Swan Lake
Photograph: K. Fischer, Moscow-St Petersburg

Vera Coralli joined the Bolshoi in 1906. She later danced with Diaghilev's company, and was Ballet Mistress in Bucharest from 1930 to 1937. She was one of the first Russian film stars.

Alexandre Volinine entered the Bolshoi in 1901 and subsequently joined Diaghilev's company. He partnered Pavlova from 1914 to 1925. He opened a school of dancing in Paris, and André Eglevsky and Renée Jeanmaire were both his pupils.

Fokines i Rosendrömmen

252
Foto: Hofatelier Jaeger, 1914.
Ensamrätt: Axel Eliassons
Konstförlag. Stockholm

a

Miss Duncan.

1174

b

Л. Г. КЯКШТЪ. (Бал. „Тщетная Предосторожн.")
M-lle Kiakscht. (Ballet: „La fille mal gardée".)

c

2863. КАРАЛЛИ и ВОЛИНИНЪ. (Бал. „Лебединое озеро".)

Собств. изданія фотогр. и худож. фотот. К. А. Фишеръ, Москва—С.-Петербургъ.

d

4a VERA CORALLI (b. Moscow, 1889; d. Vienna, 1972) as *The Dying Swan*

This ballet, to music by Saint-Saëns (from *Carnival of the Animals*), was created for Pavlova by Michel Fokine in 1907, although the dancer Lydia Kyasht always claimed that it was she who first danced the role. It is in the repertoire of all the great ballerinas, and Coralli's interpretation was particularly famous. (See also 3d)

4b LE PAVILLON D'ARMIDE

This postcard shows costumes designed by Alexandre Benois for Armide and Rinaldo in *Le Pavillon d'Armide*, a ballet in one act by Fokine with music by Nicolas Tcherepnin, first produced in 1907 at the Maryinsky Theatre, St Petersburg, with Anna Pavlova, Paul Gerdt, and Vaslav Nijinsky. The postcard is hand-coloured and was sold for the benefit of The Red Cross.

4c LAURENT NOVIKOFF (b. Moscow, 1888; d. New Buffalo, 1956) in *Autumn Bacchanale* (?)

Laurent Novikoff joined the Bolshoi in 1906. He danced with Diaghilev's company in Paris in 1909 and with Pavlova's in 1911-14, returning to the Bolshoi in 1914. He was again with Diaghilev in 1919-21, and with Pavlova from 1921-28. Well known as a teacher in London and Chicago, Novikoff was Ballet Master at the Metropolitan Opera between 1941-45. *Autumn Bacchanale* was one of the short ballets in Pavlova's repertoire and when Mordkin left the company, Novikoff danced it with her frequently.

a

b

c

Music-Hall   **5a**   MINI FISHER as the Prince in *Cinderella*
                                   Publisher: J. Baker & Son, Avondale Series
                                   Photograph: F. Bustin

The principal boy in pantomime at the turn of the century in no way tried to act or appear masculine. These performances were totally unambiguous and aimed only at revealing feminine charms in an era where the lower female extremities were seldom visible.

5b   MINNIE MIRIAM as Dandini in *Cinderella*
                  Rotary Photographic Series
                  Photograph: Whitlock, Birmingham

The pantomime artist is not as well documented as one would like. It must be remembered that every town in Great Britain had its Christmas panto, and in the larger cities there was often quite a choice. So many of the performers would inevitably have been forgotten except for the great popularity of the picture postcard, which unfortunately often gives no details concerning the artists.

5c   CARRIE MOORE (b. Geelong, Victoria, 1882; d. Sydney, 1956)
                  as Aladdin, 1905
                  Rotary Photographic Series   Photograph: R. Brown

Success came early to Carrie Moore. Discovered by J. C. Williamson at the age of fourteen, she first appeared in a pantomime spectacular *Djin-Djin* in Melbourne in 1896. At fifteen she understudied and appeared for Ada Reeve in *The French Maid*; at seventeen she was already prima donna of the Australian Royal Comic-Opera Company, and by the age of twenty had sung twenty-five leading roles, including most of the Gilbert and Sullivan heroines. In 1903 George Edwardes brought her to London. She played principal boy to Billie Burke in pantomime, and had major successes in *The Girl from Kay's*, *The Cingalee*, *Blue Moon*, *Tom Jones*, and as the Sandow Girl in *The Dairymaids*.

In 1908 she created the first Australian performances of *The Merry Widow* and married a well-known racehorse owner, returning to England in time for the Christmas pantomimes. In 1909 she played *A Persian Princess* and in 1910 toured in *Our Miss Gibbs*. She toured Australia again in 1912-13 and played in her last shows in 1917.

In 1933, when Her Majesty's in Sydney was forced to close, she impersonated herself as the Merry Widow in a tableau of famous artists who had performed in Australia, a line-up which included Nance O'Neill, Tittell-Brune, Bernhardt, Melba and Pavlova. In 1938 she appeared in the Royal Variety Performance at the London Coliseum (attended by King George VI and Queen Elizabeth), singing and dancing the new 'Lambeth Walk', with Lupino Lane, Bransby Williams, Florrie Forde, Violet and Irene Vanbrugh, Mabel Love, et al. Carrie Moore was offered roles in Hollywood during the Second World War but had to refuse because of failure to secure a work permit. In 1945 she appeared in the tiny role of the Midwife in Charles Chauvel's film *Sons of Matthew*.

5d   MARIE LOFTUS (b. Glasgow, 1857; d. 1940)
                  Publisher: Raphael Tuck & Sons   Photograph: Langner

A genuine star in the music-hall, Marie Loftus frequently appeared as a glamorous principal boy, always stunningly dressed. She made her first appearances in Glasgow in 1874 and her London début was at the Oxford in 1877. She toured America and South Africa with great success, and was known as 'the Sarah Bernhardt of the Halls' (as well as 'Kilkenny Kate'). She was part of the all-star Drury Lane pantomime of 1892 which boasted Marie Lloyd, Ada Blanche, Dan Leno, Herbert Campbell, Little Tich and Mabel Love. She was the mother of actress Cissie Loftus, who at various times appeared in the company of Martin Harvey, Helena Modjeska, Henry Irving, E. H. Sothern and William Faversham.

MISS MINI FISHER,
AS THE PRINCE IN CINDERELLA.

COPYRIGHT, 69.   J. BAKER & SON.

a

11460 A   MISS MINNIE MIRIAM.   ROTARY PHOTO. E.C
AS "DANDINI" IN "CINDERELLA"

b

1799 J   MISS CARRIE MOORE.   ROTARY PHOTO. E.C.

c

The "VARIETY" Stage.   MARIE LOFTUS.

d

6a   WILLIAM SYDNEY PENLEY (b. Margate, 1852; d. 1912) as
                Charley's Aunt'
                Publisher: T. C. Turner   Rotary Photo   Autographed

In the first London production of the three-act farce *Charley's Aunt* by Brandon Thomas, W. S. Penley created the title role of Lord Fancourt Babberley, who masquerades as the aunt from Brazil, 'where the nuts come from'. This perennial favourite opened at the Royalty Theatre on 21 October 1892, transferring to the Globe on 30 January 1893 where it continued until April 1896, realising almost 1500 performances. It has been revived constantly, in countless languages, ever since.

Penley began his acting career in the early 'seventies in the burlesques so favoured at the time (his début being in a farce called *Zampa* in 1871 at the Court Theatre), progressing to comic opera and straight plays. In 1875 he was much praised in D'Oyly Carte's original run of *Trial by Jury*, playing the Foreman, and later the Judge which he took over on the death of the composer's brother, Frederic Sullivan. Further London appearances included *Princess Toto*, *Crutch and Toothpick*, and *Falka*, with his first long-running success coming in 1884 when he succeeded Beerbohm Tree as the Rev. Robert Spalding in Charles Hawtrey's farce *The Private Secretary*, an adaptation of von Moser's *Der Bibliotheker*. In 1900 Penley opened the Great Queen Street Theatre (formerly the Novelty) but retired from the stage the following year. His mournful, deadpan delivery and sorrowful features contrasted comically with the zany farcical lines of many of his roles.

6b   HARRY FRAGSON (see 7c), HARRY RANDALL (1860-1932),
                FRED EMNEY SR (1865-1917) and WALTER PASSMORE
                (1867-1946) in *Sinbad*
                Publisher: Raphael Tuck & Sons, 'Play Pictorial Series'
                Photograph: Dover Street Studios   Postmark: 7 February 1907

Sinbad, the Drury Lane panto of 1906-07, had an all-star cast, even by the sumptuous standards of Drury Lane pantomimes.

Harry Randall made his first panto appearance in 1871. He appeared in all the leading music-halls in Britain for thirty years, writing many of his own songs, and performed at Drury Lane for five years – playing both male and 'dame' parts.

Fred Emney Sr in 1885 appeared in *The Forty Thieves* with Nelly Farren, with whom he also played in *Aladdin*. He played Arthur Lurcher in *Dorothy* some 800 times in 1887-89. After many years of light opera and musical comedy he moved to the halls. He was often the 'dame' in the Drury Lane pantomimes.

Walter Passmore began in pantomime in 1881. He acted at the Savoy from 1893 to 1903; there, as the successor to George Grossmith, he played all the Gilbert and Sullivan roles for which he became famous – KoKo, Jack Point, Don Alhambra, Sir Joseph Porter and Bunthorne. He took part in the Drury Lane pantos of 1905-07 and subsequently toured in variety. He appeared in *The Rebel Maid* at the Empire in 1921, *Our Nell* at the Gaiety in 1924, and in a gala performance of *Trial by Jury* at His Majesty's in 1927.

6c   DAN LENO (b. 1860; d. 1904) as Sister Anne in *Bluebeard*
                her: Raphael Tuck & Sons, 'Artists in their Dressing Room'
                Series

A greatly beloved star of English music-hall and pantomime, Dan Leno appeared for years in the Drury Lane pantomimes – as Widow Twankey, Mother Goose, Sister Anne, the Baroness and Cinderella's step-mother. He was known as the 'Garrick of the Halls' and, after a Command Performance for Edward VII, 'The King's Jester'. His mind failed him towards the end of a relatively short life and unprecedented crowds attended his funeral.

6d   GEORGE ROBEY (b. 1869; d. 1954) in *The Queen of Hearts*
                Rotary Photographic Series   Hand-coloured

A star of music-hall and pantomime, nearly always in a bowler hat and with enormous bushy eyebrows (when not playing a 'dame'), George Robey appeared in practically every music hall of note in Britain. In films he played Sancho Panza to Chaliapin's Don Quixote, and Falstaff to Olivier's Henry V. The reviews in which he appeared with Violet Loraine, *The Bing Boys are Here* and *The Bing Boys on Broadway*, were enormously popular.

He was created a Knight of the British Empire, and was known as the 'Prime Minister of Mirth'.

127a T. C. TURNER
London & Hull.
W. S. PENLEY
(CHARLEY'S AUNT)
ROTARY PHOTO, E.C.

a

SINDBAD (DRURY LANE PANTOMIME, 1907)   5292
EMPRESS OF SAHARA (MR. FRED EMNEY)
ENVOY (MR. HARRY FRAGSON)
MRS. SINDBAD (MR. HARRY RANDALL)
SINDBAD (MR. WALTER PASSMORE)

b

MR. DAN LENO.

c

4237 H
MR. GEORGE ROBEY,
"THE QUEEN OF HEARTS."
ROTARY PHOTO, E.C.

d

7a   MARIE LLOYD (b. 1870; d. 1922)
          Publisher: J. Beagles & Co., London
          Photograph: Ellis & Walery   Autographed

'Our Marie', legendary music-hall artiste, was the eldest of nine children and made her début in 1885. Although she was accused of lewdness her songs were really quite innocent – it was her delicious sense of innuendo which suggested unthought-of meanings. A wittily vulgar but not coarse performer, she was beloved by her public for her spirit, courage and compulsive generosity.

She appeared for years in the Drury Lane pantomimes. Sarah Bernhardt was known to have said that she was the only woman of genius on the English stage.

7b   CICELY COURTNEIDGE (b. Sydney, 1893; d. 1980) in *The Pearl Girl*
          Rotary Photographic Series
          Photograph: Foulsham & Banfield, London   Autographed

It was in the production of *The Pearl Girl* that Cicely Courtneidge met her husband Jack Hulbert, whom she married in 1915; the marriage lasted for over sixty years, seeing them through many times both on and off the stage. She was the daughter of the impressario Robert Courtneidge and first appeared as Peasblossom in *A Midsummer Night's Dream* at the age of eight.

She began as a performer in musical comedy and progressed through many revues and variety performances, films and straight plays until a ripe old age. Her name was synonymous with *vitality* and she made her last stage appearance in 1976. She was created a Dame of the British Empire in 1972 for services to the theatre.

7c   HARRY FRAGSON (b. 1869; d. 1913)
          Photograph: J. Davey, London   Autographed

An Anglo-French music-hall artist (whose real name was Potts), Harry Fragson was equally at home on both sides of the Channel – with a Cockney accent in Paris and a French one in London. He was the first of the music-hall singers to accompany himself at the piano. His death was pure *Grand Guignol*: he was shot by his own father during a fit of insanity.

7d   EUGENE STRATTON (b. 1861; d. 1918)
          Rotary Photographic Series   Photograph: Whitlock

The American-born music-hall performer Eugene Stratton came to England with Haverley's Minstrels in 1880 and joined the Moore-Burgess Minstrels in 1881, remaining with them until 1892 when he took to the halls alone, appearing first at the Royal Holborn in that year. He was said to be the finest of all the coon singers (as they were then known), the most popular of all the black-face performers. 'Lily of Laguna' was one of his most popular songs.

452 H.
J. BEAGLES & CO.   MISS MARIE LLOYD.   ELLIS & WALERY.

a

6922 N ROTARY PHOTO, E.C.   MISS CICELY COURTNEIDGE   FOULSHAM & BANFIELD, LTD., W.
AS "LADY BETTY BIDDULPH" IN "THE PEARL GIRL"

b

10971 G.
W. DAVEY, PHOTO.   HARRY FRAGSON.   UPPER ST., N.

c

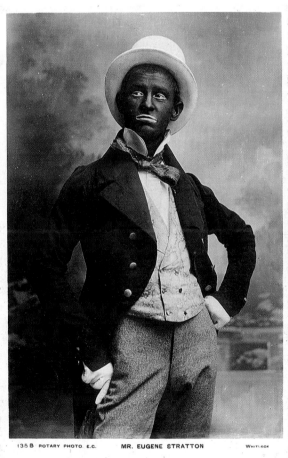

135 B ROTARY PHOTO, E.C.   MR. EUGENE STRATTON   WHITLOCK

d

8a   LIANE DE POUGY (b. La Flèche, 1869; d. Lausanne, 1950)
          Publisher: SIP, Paris   Photograph: Reutlinger, Paris
          Hand-coloured

Liane de Pougy was one of the great courtesans of the *belle époque*. Educated in a convent and married at the age of sixteen, she soon left her husband and ran away to Paris. Her extraordinary beauty opened the doors of the Folies-Bergère, the Théâtre Michel in St Petersburg and the Palace Theatre in London. She appeared as Metella in Offenbach's *La Vie Parisienne* and Venus in his *Orphée aux Enfers*. She was the mistress of many rich and famous men, and her houses, carriages and jewels were greatly envied. After twenty years of this life she married a penniless Romanian aristocrat, Prince Georges Ghika. She began her memoirs in 1919 and continued writing them until 1941.

Towards the end of her life she entered a community of nuns in Switzerland as Soeur Marie-Madeleine, and ended her life in extreme piety tending the needs of abnormal children.

8b   CLÉO DE MÉRODE (b. circa 1873; d. ?)
          Publisher: SIP, Paris   Photograph: Reutlinger, Paris
          Hand-coloured

Born in Paris of Viennese parents, Cléo de Mérode was accepted by the Opéra dance class at seven and had a career as a classical dancer in Paris, Hamburg, Berlin, St Petersburg, Budapest and New York. In this latter city she appeared in a three-act ballet, *Faust*, and in 1901 first appeared at the Folies-Bergère in a three-act ballet, *Lorenza*.

Remembered less as a dancer than as a great beauty, with flawless skin, she was one of the famed courtesans of her day and the mistress of King Leopold II of the Belgians. She performed her own specialty dances – oriental, Spanish, Greek or gypsy – in the music-halls. When the sculptor Farquière exhibited a nude statue of her, she revelled in the subsequent publicity.

8c   GABY DESLYS (b. Marseilles, circa 1881; d. Paris, 1920)
          Signed: Palmer-Jones

This is an advertising card for André Charlot's *5064 Gerrard* at the Alhambra Theatre in London, 1915.

With her ample figure and cute blond looks, Gaby Deslys was a huge success in Parisian revue from her début in 1902; she appeared at the Parisiana, Les Matharins, the Marigny, the Scala and the Olympia. In 1906 she made a London début at the Gaiety in *The New Aladdin*, and in 1910 had the title role in *Les Caprices de Suzette* at the Alhambra. She had many successes in London at the Wintergarden, the Palace and the Duke of York's.

Gaby Deslys was a great success in the Irving Berlin revue *Stop, Look and Listen* in New York in 1915. Her great beauty and naughty Parisian reputation made her the darling of the press and public. The American dancer Harry Pilcer was her frequent partner. She appeared at the Folies-Bergère and introduced American ragtime to Paris.

8d   LA BELLE OTERO (b. Barcelona, 1868; d. Nice, 1965)
          Publisher: SIP, Paris   Photograph: Reutlinger, Paris

Caroline Otero ran away from home aged twelve or thirteen and found herself jobs singing and dancing in cafés and music-halls in between her frequent love affairs. Like her rivals Cléo de Mérode and Liane de Pougy, she became more famous off her feet than on them.

She made her way to the Folies-Bergère in Paris in 1889, when she triumphed season after season – her bosom covered with her own very real jewels. Her triumphs took her to Moscow and St Petersburg, most of the great cities of Europe, and North and South America.

Her lovers included the kings of England, Serbia and Spain, the Kaiser, the Russian Grand Dukes, Peter and Nicholas, the Duke of Westminster and Gabriele d'Annunzio. Men fought duels over her and blew their brains out because of her. Her breasts were so famous that the twin cupolas of the Hotel Carlton in Cannes were modelled after them.

During her acting life she made fortunes which she impulsively gambled away. She entertained the troops throughout the First World War and then suddenly retired with her fame and beauty intact. She lived on in the south of France, ever more dignified as she became poorer and poorer. She died at the age of ninety-seven, forty-seven years after retiring from her extraordinary life.

a

b

c

d

9a   JULIAN ELTINGE (b. Massachusetts, 1882; d. New York, 1941)
          Publisher: GG Co.   Photograph: Gerlach

The most famous American female impersonator of his day, 'Mr Lillian Russell' was reputed never to be vulgar. His first appearance as a female was with the Boston cadets, aged ten. He appeared at the Palace Theatre in London in 1906 and at the Alhambra in New York in 1907, but his career was really launched by *The Fascinating Widow* at the Liberty Theatre, New York, in which he played the dual roles of Mrs Monte and Mr Blake.

A performer of some subtlety, he wore beautiful gowns and had a good voice. His bathing beauty sketch was particularly popular. He made a few silent films but by the end of the First World War his age and weight began to tell; nevertheless, he continued in vaudeville through the 'thirties and made his last appearance in Billy Rose's *Diamond Horseshoe Jubilee* in 1940.

9b   ROBERT STEIDL
          Photograph: Zander & Labisch

This card shows the German revue artist, Robert Steidl, as a Spanish dancer at the Apollo Theatre, Berlin – the locale of many spectacular revues and circuses. Many of the great musical spectaculars of the once-famous Paul Lincke (remembered for *The Glow-Worm Idyll*) were performed here.

9c   HETTY KING (b. 1883; d. 1972)
          Rotary Photo   Hand-coloured

On the stage for over seventy years, the male impersonator Hetty King amused her public with 'All the nice girls love a sailor', 'I do make a hit with the ladies', 'When a fellah is twenty-one' and 'Piccadilly'.

She made her début in 1897 at the London Music Hall in Shoreditch, and topped the bill throughout Britain and America. Her vitality was truly enviable and she continued to perform even when approaching the age of ninety.

9d   VESTA TILLEY (b. 1864; d. 1952)
          Rotary Photo
          Photograph: Brown, Barnes & Bell, Liverpool

A variety performer from childhood, the 'Great Little Tilley', the 'Pocket Sims Reeves' (after the great tenor), and finally, the 'London Idol', spent most of her life on stage as a male impersonator. The public adored her as cheeky soldiers and sailors during the Boer War, in tails and white tie, as a page boy, a clergyman, or a judge. She dispensed with the corsets and tights which were *de rigeur* at the time, and her trim little figure fascinated Britain and the United States for over fifty years. Off-stage Vesta Tilley was the elegant and charming wife of a Member of Parliament, and she eventually became Lady de Freece.

She had a great celebration at the Coliseum in 1920 to say farewell to an adoring public, and retired with her husband to Monte Carlo.

a

b

c

d

10a   MLLE REY
              Photograph: Walery, Paris   Hand-coloured

This postcard shows Mlle Rey as a rather saucy bullfighter in some long-forgotten Parisian revue.

10b   EVE DE MILO
              Photograph: Walery, Paris   Hand-coloured

A 'naughty' picture from the Folies-Bergère. Mlle de Milo is rather ample by today's pulchritudinous standards.

10c   LOUISE WILLY (b. 1873; d. 1954)
              Publisher: Papier Guilleminot
              Photograph: Stebbing, Paris   Hand-coloured

After divorcing her husband the author-critic, 'Willy' (Henri Gauthier-Villars), Louise Willy – later known to the world as Colette – spent six years in the music-halls of Paris. She became one of the greatest of all French writers, and apart from her wonderful reminiscences is best known to the general public as the author of *Gigi*, *Chéri*, *The Last of Chéri* and the *Claudine* novels.

10d   MLLE DE MORLAIX

Here we see Mlle de Morlaix of the Théâtre du Gaité-Rochechouart, another of the splendid little revue theatres of the *belle époque*. This card is hand-coloured and stamped on the back 'Sole Agent, Macropolo, Calcutta'.

a

b

c

d

Circus   **11a**   ANITA & THE BARONESS IRMGARD

Two midgets from the Siebold & Herhaus Märchenschau. This card is postmarked Pforzheim, 20 June 1927.

The little people have always held great fascination for those of normal height. They themselves seem to be fascinated by aristocratic titles – or perhaps the aristocracy is prone to giving birth to midgets. In circus and variety annals we find the names of Princess Nouma-Hawa, Princess Dot, Princess Chinquilla, Duchesse Léone Migeot, King Lilliput, Prince Colibri, Prince Smaun Singh Hpoo, Prince Atom, Baron Nicolas de Burcey, Little Lord Roberts, not to mention quite a collection of majors, generals and commodores.

11b   HARRY HOUDINI (b. Budapest, 1873; d. 1926)
           Publisher: Nordische Kunstanstalt, Ernst Schmidt & Co.,
           Lübeck   Autographed: 18 February 1914

The famous escapologist and magician was born Ehrich Weiss in Budapest, but went to the United States as a child. In 1900 he persuaded the police of Scotland Yard to handcuff him to a pillar; his escape was instantaneous – as was his fame.

Billed as 'The King of Handcuffs' and 'The Monarch of Leg Shackles', Houdini kept the vaudeville public entertained for years, making his escape while manacled or straight-jacketed – from under water, from coffins, from gaols, from under frozen rivers, etc. He appeared in several silent films, and movies of his life were made in 1943 (with Tony Curtis) and in 1976 (for television, with Paul Michael Glaser).

Strangely enough, it was his slow reaction to unexpected punches in the abdomen by a student testing his ability to withstand injury that caused his death from peritonitis several days after the incident.

11c   GROCK (b. Switzerland, 1880; d. 1959)
           Photograph: Dix, Paris

The Swiss Adrien Wettach, known as Grock, was the greatest clown of his generation. He appeared throughout Europe in circus and music-hall. His first English appearance was at the Palace Theatre, London, in 1911 and he played there for many years. A great mime, adept at tragi-comedy, he made silent films in England and Germany.

11d   PAUL CINQUEVALLI (b. 1859; d. 1918)
           Publisher: London Sterio Company   Photograph: Rotary
           Date on reverse: 1906

The great Polish juggler, Paul Cinquevalli (born Paul Kestner) ran away as a child to join the circus and became a trapeze artist. However, a fall in St Petersburg, after which he spent ten months in hospital, brought his trapeze days to an end. He turned to juggling – which he brought to a fine art. He made a London début in a circus at Covent Garden in 1885 and first appeared in the United States in 1888. He toured Australia, South Africa, India and South America, but made London his home. He was a star personality and appeared at the first Royal Command Performance at the Palace Theatre in 1912. He retired in 1915 and died in London.

Siebold & Herhaus Märchenschau: Anita und Baroness Irmgard

a

Harry Houdini

b

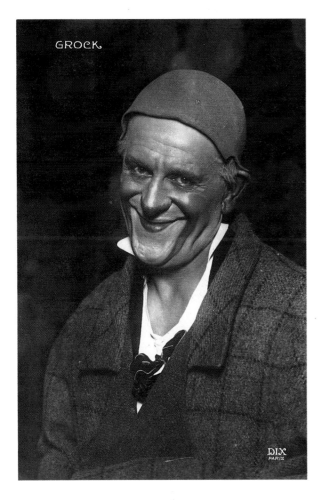

GROCK

DIX
PARIS

c

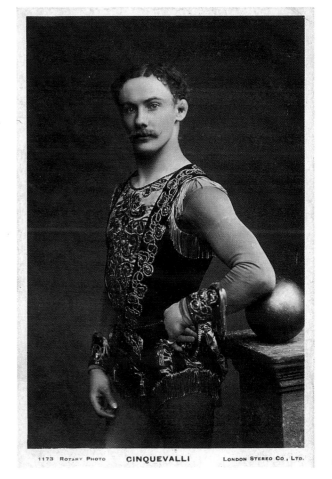

1173 Rotary Photo CINQUEVALLI London Stereo Co., Ltd.

d

12a   LES ROUBAIX DUO
                 Photograph: Louys Bauer, Dijon

A French acrobatic and trapeze duo who performed early in this century.

12b   'AUS DEM ZIRCUS'
                 Publisher: Aquarell Künstlerkarten von L. Fränzl, Munich
                 Postmark: 9 December 1901, Paris

A souvenir of the Barnum and Bailey circus, 'The Greatest Show on Earth'.

12c   FAMILIE BIRKENEDER

These were German circus athletes at the turn of the century. The child of five years is billed as the smallest athlete in the world and able to lift 450 pounds.

12d   LA FAMILLE D'ESQUIMAUX

The card shows Madame Stella, 36 years old and 71 cm in height; her daughter, Miss Corabella, 16 years and 60 cm, and her son, Prince Mignon, age 13 and 50 cm. This 'Eskimo' family (?) of midgets with the fancy names appeared in French circuses early in this century.

LES ROUBAIX, duo

Merveilleux travail de Voltige

LOUYS BAUER, PHOTOTYPIE, DIJON.

a

Souvenir from the

Barnum & Bailey

Greatest Show on Earth

b

Familie Birkeneder, Salonathleten

Der kleinste Athlet der Welt ist 5 Jahre alt und trägt 450 Pfund.

c

SOUVENIR DE LA FAMILLE D'ESQUIMAUX

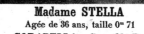

Madame STELLA

Agée de 36 ans, taille 0ᵐ 71

Sa fille Miss CORABELLA   Son fils Prince MIGNON

Agée de 16 ans, taille 0ᵐ 60   Agé de 13 ans, taille 0ᵐ 50

d

13a   FAMILLE ROBBA

This splendid couple are surely circus athletes of some sort, but I have found no information covering them. Lack of knowledge never stops me from buying an amusing or beautiful card – the required information frequently turns up years later and leads one into yet another path.

13b   THE FIVE ORIGINAL CLIFTONS
                 Publisher: Schmidt & Gebr. Böttger, Lübeck

The name Clifton occurs many times in literature concerning variety performers, but I have yet to find any information on the Five Originals. They were probably touring in Germany when this photo was taken.

13c   SOUVENIR DU CIRQUE VARIÉTÉS, LIÈGE
                 Publisher: W. Biede, Nuremberg
                 Postmark: 13 January 1902, Liège

A souvenir printed for the opening of the Cirque Variétés in Liège, 1 September 1900.

Famille ROBBA

a

The 5 Original Cliftons

b

c

Cinema   **14a**   GARY COOPER (b. 1901; d. 1961)
                           Valentine's Post Card (circa 1934)   Hand-coloured

Printed on the reverse of the postcard is this early résumé: 'This brilliant Paramount Star began work as a newspaper cartoonist with ambitions towards commercial art. He is 33 years of age. He has scored many successes on the screen, and has appeared opposite many famous Stars amongst whom are Helen Hayes, Tallulah Bankhead, Claudette Colbert, and Carole Lombard. He was born at Helena, came to England at 10 years of age and was educated at Dunstable School'.

   The American film actor Gary Cooper made films from 1925 until his death in 1961, and was awarded a special Academy Award in 1960 'for his many memorable screen performances and for the international recognition he as an individual, has gained for the film industry'. His notable films include *A Farewell to Arms* (1932), *Lives of a Bengal Lancer* (1935), *Mr Deeds Goes to Town* (1936), *Beau Geste* (1939), *Sergeant York* (1941), *For Whom the Bell Tolls* (1943) and *High Noon* (1952).

14b   CHARLIE CHAPLIN (b. 1889; d. 1977)
              Valentine's 'Real Photograph' Series

The legendary British clown-tramp of the cinema, Charlie Chaplin, was beloved by his public the world over but alienated many people in private life. He began making silent movies in 1914 and most of his output preceded the 'talkies', notably: *Tillie's Punctured Romance* (1914), *The Tramp* (1915), *The Kid* (1920), *The Gold Rush* (1924), *The Circus* (1928) and *City Lights* (1931). His most significant 'talkies' were *Modern Times* (1936), *The Great Dictator* (1940), *Monsieur Verdoux* (1947) and *Limelight* (1952).

   Charlie Chaplin received an honorary Academy Award in 1971 and was knighted by Her Majesty Queen Elizabeth II in 1975. He is author of four autobiographical books, written between 1922 and 1974, and the subject of numerous biographies.

14c   CHARLES BOYER (b. 1899; d. 1978)
              Publisher: R.K.O. Radio

The French film actor Charles Boyer, was known as the 'great lover': he was the epitome of the romantic Frenchman to his British and American fans. He began with silent films in France in 1920, came to Hollywood in 1929, and continued to make feminine hearts flutter until the mid-'seventies. As well as having great charm, he was also a fine actor. His films include *The Garden of Allah* (1936), *Mayerling* (1937), *All This and Heaven Too* (1940), *Gaslight* (1944), *Fanny* (1962) and *Barefoot in the Park* (1968).

14d   ROBERT TAYLOR (b. 1911; d. 1969)
              Publisher: Metro-Goldwyn Mayer

The handsome American actor Robert Taylor made his first film in 1934 and continued in the movies until 1968. Among his fine films are *Magnificent Obsession* (1935), *Broadway Melody* (1936), *Camille* (1936), *A Yank at Oxford* (1938), *Waterloo Bridge* (1940), *Johnny Eager* (1941) and *Quo Vadis* (1951). Although he was never what could be called a great actor, Robert Taylor's popularity was immense. His earlier films are far superior to the later ones.

GARY COOPER (Paramount) 59041

a

CHARLIE CHAPLIN
CINEMA STAR.

b

CHARLES BOYER   R.K.O. RADIO

c

ROBERT TAYLOR   METRO-GOLDWYN-MAYER
PICTURES

d

15a   RENEE ADOREE and RAMON NOVARRO in *Call of the*
               Flesh (1930)
               Publisher: Verlag 'Ross', Berlin
               Photograph: Metro-Goldwyn-Mayer

Renée Adorée (1898-1933), the exquisite French star, went from the circus to the silent films; illness terminated her career and she did not make the transfer to the 'talkies'. *The Big Parade* (1925) with John Gilbert was the film which made her famous. She also appeared in *La Bohème* (1926), *Forbidden Hours* (1928), *The Pagan* (1929), *The Spoiler* (1929) and *Call of the Flesh* (1930).
      Ramon Novarro: see **16a**.

15b   GLORIA SWANSON and RUDOLPH VALENTINO in
               Beyond the Rocks (1922)
               Publisher: Verlag 'Ross', Berlin   Photograph: Paramount

Gloria Swanson (1897-1983), the American actress, began her cinematic life as a Mack Sennett bathing beauty in 1915 and made many silent films – a series of them for De Mille, many for Paramount and several for United Artists, including *Sadie Thompson* (1928).
      The English novelist Elinor Glyn wrote the film *Beyond the Rocks* especially for Swanson and Valentino, with flashbacks so that they could appear in romantic clothes of a different era. She wrote in her fanciful style of Swanson: 'I feel she has an old soul struggling to remember its former lives – not young like the great America'.
      Gloria Swanson rarely appeared in sound films, but made a brilliant comeback in *Sunset Boulevard* in 1950, in which she starred with William Holden and Erich von Stroheim.
      Rudolph Valentino: see **16b**.

15c   ANTON WALBROOK and ANNA NEAGLE in *Victoria the*
               Great (1937)
               'Film Partners' Series, London
               Photograph: R.K.O. Radio   Hand-coloured

Anton Walbrook (1900-67) was an Austrian actor who came to England before the war and began making films in 1935. His notable films, in addition to the above, are *The Life and Death of Colonel Blimp* (1943), *The Red Shoes* (1948), *The Queen of Spades* (1948) and *La Ronde* (1950).
      Anna Neagle (1904-86) was one of Britain's best loved actresses of stage and screen; she was married to producer Herbert Wilcox. She will be remembered for her many historical portrayals on film – Queen Victoria, Nurse Edith Cavell, Peg Woffington, Nell Gwynn, Amy Johnson, Odette and Florence Nightingale – and she also made some charming comedies with Michael Wilding.
      In the last two decades of her life Anna Neagle returned to the stage. She was created a Dame of the British Empire.

15d   RONALD COLMAN and VILMA BANKY in *The Night of*
               Love (1927)
               Publisher: J. Beagles & Co., 'Famous Cinema Star' Series
               Photograph: Allied Artists

Vilma Banky (b. circa 1898) was an Austro-Hungarian vamp of the silent films. Her first films were made in Hungary, and later in Germany, France and Austria (1920-25), before Sam Goldwyn brought her to America to make *The Dark Angel* in 1925. She appeared in *The Eagle* (1925) and *The Son of the Sheik* (1926) with Rudolph Valentino. The following year she married actor Rod la Rocque, with whom she made the sound film *This Is Heaven* in 1929 and toured America with *Cherries Are Ripe*. In 1932 she went to Germany with La Rocque where she made her last film.
      Ronald Colman (1891-1958), the romantic British film actor, began in the silent films in 1919 and continued into the 'talkies', in which he worked until his death in 1958. Many of his performances continue to enchant, notably those in *A Tale of Two Cities* (1935), *The Prisoner of Zenda* (1937), *Random Harvest* (1942) and *A Double Life* (1948), for which he won an Academy Award.

Renée Adorée — Ramon Novarro

„Ross" Verlag   Reproduction verboten   **a**

Gloria Swanson — Rudolph Valentino

Verlag „Ross" Berlin SW 68.   **b**

ANTON WALBROOK AND ANNA NEAGLE   **c**

RONALD COLMAN & VILMA BANKY in "The Night of Love". 'FAMOUS CINEMA STAR' SERIES   **d**

16a   RAMON NOVARRO (b. 1899; d. 1968) as Ben Hur
Cinémagazine-Edition, Paris   Photograph: R. Morgan

A heart-throb of the silent film era from 1916, the Mexican Ramon Novarro starred in films such as *The Prisoner of Zenda* (1922), *Scaramouche* (1923), *Ben Hur* (1925) and *The Student Prince* (1927). In the 'talkies' *Mata Hari* (1931), *The Barbarian* (1933) and *The Sheik Steps Out* (1937) he was less successful, but he continued as a character actor into the 'fifties and 'sixties. He was found naked in his villa, assassinated, in 1968.

16b   RUDOLPH VALENTINO (b. 1895; d. 1926) in *The Son of the Sheik* (1926)
Publisher: J. Beagles & Co., 'Famous Cinema Star' Series
Photograph: Paramount

The Italian-American 'lady-killer' of the silent films, Rudolph Valentino, had a magnetic and almost hypnotic personality which made him the great matinee idol of his day. His films – all silent – are still riveting, notably *The Four Horsemen of the Apocalypse* (1921), *The Sheik* (1921), *Blood and Sand* (1922), *The Young Rajah* (1922), *Monsieur Beaucaire* (1924), *A Sainted Devil* (1924), *The Eagle* (1925), *The Cobra* (1925) and *The Son of the Sheik* (1926). In the latter film, which was showing at the time of his death, the heroine was Vilma Banky.

16c   RICHARD BARTHLEMESS (b. 1895; d. 1963)
Publisher: Förlag Nordisk Konst, Stockholm

Richard Barthlemess was a leading man of the silent films from 1916 onwards; many of the films in which he starred were directed by D. W. Griffith. He appeared in more than fifty films, including *Broken Blossoms* with Lillian Gish (1918), *Tol'able David* (1921), *The Patent Leather Kid* (1927), *The Dawn Patrol* (1930), *Cabin in the Cotton* (1932) and *Only Angels Have Wings* (1939). He made the transition to sound films, which he continued to make until the 'forties, mainly as a character actor.

16d   JOHN BARRYMORE (b. 1882; d. 1942) in *Don Juan* (1926)

The younger son of handsome actor Maurice Barrymore, and brother to Ethel and Lionel, 'The Great Profile' was a matinee idol of both stage and screen. From 1913 onwards he made many silent films, and he continued making films and acting on stage until his death. He had major successes in New York on stage, in Tolstoi's *Redemption* and in Shakespeare's *Richard III* and *Hamlet*, in which he had a very long run and which he repeated successfully in London. A very fine actor early in his career, he degenerated into quite a ham in later life, overtaken by alcoholism.

a

b

c

d

17a   POLA NEGRI (b. circa 1894; d. 1987)
            Publisher: Cinémagazine, Paris

Pola Negri, the Polish actress of stage and screen, trained at the Imperial Ballet School in St Petersburg and made her stage and film débuts in Warsaw in 1913-14. Encouraged by Max Reinhardt she went to Berlin in 1917; there she received high praise for her stage performances in *Sumurun*, playing opposite Emil Jannings and with fellow actor Ernst Lubitsch. Between 1918 and 1920 she made several films in Germany, many under the direction of Lubitsch; *Carmen* (re-named *Gypsy Love*) and *Du Barry* (re-named *Passion*), with Emil Jannings, were the most successful.

In 1922 Pola Negri arrived in America where she became the epitome of the 'vamp'. Among her early American films are: *La Bella Donna* (1923), *Forbidden Paradise* (1924) directed by Lubitsch, *Lily of the Dust* (1924), *Shadows of Paris* (1924), *East of Suez* (1925), *Flower of the Night* (1925), *A Woman of the World* (1925), *Hotel Imperial* (1927), *Barbed Wire* (1927) and *Loves of an Actress* (1928). She made only a few sound films, among them *Madame Bovary* (1937) and a comeback in *The Moonspinners* in 1964.

She had a much publicised affair with Rudolph Valentino, and marriages with Count Domski and Prince Mdivani. Her autobiography *Memories of a Star* was written in 1969 in San Antonio, where she lived for many years.

17b   MARY PICKFORD (b. 1893; d. 1979)
            Publisher: Cinémagazine, Paris

Mary Pickford, 'The World's Sweetheart', was one of the great silent stars; she was also a very astute woman and the business brains behind United Artists. She began acting as a child and made her first film in 1909. *Daddy Long-Legs* (1919), *Pollyanna* (1920), *Little Lord Fauntleroy* (1921), *Little Annie Rooney* (1925), and *Coquette* (1929), for which she received an Academy Award, are amongst her more enduring films. She retired shortly after the advent of sound film, but not from her business activities. Married to Douglas Fairbanks, and then to Charles 'Buddy' Rogers, she was one of America's richest women.

17c   MABEL NORMAND (b. 1894; d. 1930)
            Publisher: J. Beagles & Co., London   Hand-coloured

Mabel Normand was a comedienne of over a hundred silent films from 1911, a great many for Mack Sennett at Biograph and Keystone, and the co-star of Charlie Chaplin and Fatty Arbuckle. Although she directed a series of comedies (*Mabel's Stormy Love Affair*, *Mabel's Bare Escape*, etc), it was her pert blond looks that kept her in films rather than any intellectual ability. Her private life was fairly exotic, and the scandal of her drug-taking and involvement in the murder of director William Desmond Taylor ruined her career.

17d   ALLA NAZIMOVA (b. 1879; d. 1945)
            Publisher: J. Beagles & Co. Ltd, London   Hand-coloured

A great Russian stage actress who was already a leading lady in St Petersburg in 1904, Alla Nazimova was considered a major interpreter of Ibsen and Chekhov. The Thirty-Ninth Street Theatre in New York was renamed the Nazimova. In 1931 she created the part of the murderous Christine Mannon in Eugene O'Neill's *Mourning Becomes Elektra*. She made many American films, including *The Red Lantern* (1919), *Camille* (1921) with Valentino, *A Doll's House* (1922) and *Salome* (1923). Later in sound films she continued to entrance: in *Escape* (1940), *Blood and Sand* (1941) and *The Bridge of San Louis Rey* (1944).

POLA NEGRI

239

a

322

MARY PICKFORD

b

BEAGLES' POSTCARDS. MISS MABEL NORMAND. 102.A.
FAMOUS CINEMA STAR SERIES.

c

PHOTO: NAZIMOVA. 207.C.
JURY'S. 'FAMOUS CINEMA STAR' SERIES. BEAGLES' POSTCARDS.

d

18a   DOLORES DEL RIO (b. 1905; d. 1983)
             Photograph: Fox   Hand-coloured

This beautiful Mexican actress first appeared in silent films in 1925, and continued making films until the 'sixties. She made *The Loves of Carmen* (1927), *Resurrection* (1927), *Ramona* (1928), *Bird of Paradise* (1932) and *In Caliente* (1935). She remained a remarkable beauty well into old age.

18b   MARCELLA ALBANI (b. Rome, circa 1899; d. 1959)
             Publisher: 'Ross', Berlin
             Photograph: Atelier Schneider, Berlin

The exotic Italian actress Marcella Albani began her screen career in 1919 in Italy, where she made some twenty films which established her in the public favour. Troubles in the Italian film industry drove her to Germany, where she made almost thirty pictures between 1923 and 1936. She filmed also in France, Austria and Czechoslovakia. These films included *Russia-1908* (1929), *Behind the Altar* (1929), *The Fight for Matterhorn* (1929), *Theatre* (1929), *Secrets of the Orient* (1934), *Stradivarius* (1935) with Gustav Frölich, and *The Emperor of California* (1936),

She made the transition to sound rather badly and took to writing romantic novels after her retirement from the screen. Two of these novels were filmed: *Ritorna All Terra* (1934) in which she starred and which was directed by her husband Mario Franchini, and *Liebelei und Liebe* (1938), filmed in Germany.

18c   ELISABETH BERGNER (b. circa 1897; d. 1986)
             Publisher: 'Ross', Berlin

The German (Polish-born) actress Elisabeth Bergner began her career playing Ophelia to Moissi's Hamlet, aged nineteen, and during the late 'twenties and early 'thirties worked on the stage with Max Reinhardt (*Peer Gynt* and *St Joan*) in Germany, where she also made several silent films.

With her husband, the Hungarian film director Paul Czinner, she came to England in 1933; in England she appeared on the stage and in some splendid films, notably *Catherine the Great* (1934), *Escape Me Never* (1935) for which she won an Academy Award, and *As You Like It* (1936) with Laurence Olivier. She played Shakespeare, Ibsen, Shaw, O'Neill, Barrie, et al, in the theatre on both sides of the Atlantic, and her tours took her as far as Australia.

18d   LILLIAN GISH (b. 1896)
             'Picturegoer' Series, London   Photograph: Apeda, New York

On the reverse, in Miss Gish's handwriting, is written: 'No, I must play in Uncle Tom's Cabin. Thank you for your nice letter. Sincerely, Lillian Gish'.

One of the great monuments of the screen – her early films, directed by D. W. Griffith, were milestones of the silent era: *Birth of a Nation* (1914), *Intolerance* (1916), *Broken Blossoms* (1918), *Way Down East* (1920), *Orphans of the Storm* (1922), *La Bohème* (1926).

She continued to make appearances in films, notably *Duel in the Sun* (1946) and *Night of the Hunter* (1955), and appeared on stage through the 1970s. In 1986 she was honoured on television in New York (where she lives) by many of the big performers of today, and at the age of ninety was more mobile, more coherent, and more beautiful than many actresses a great deal younger than she.

Dolores Del Rio

a

Marcella Albani

1926.

b

Elisabeth Bergner

Verlag „Ross" Berlin SW 68.

c

LILLIAN GISH.

d

19a   LILIAN HARVEY (b. London, 1906; d. Antibes, 1968)
Publisher: 'Ross', Berlin   Photograph: UFA

The blonde English actress, dancer and singer, Lilian Harvey, went to Germany before the First World War and there became a star of comedies and musical film throughout the 'thirties. Her popularity was immense and many of her pictures were made in several languages. Of particular interest are her films for UFA: *Liebeswalzer* (1929), *Der Kongress Tanzt* (1931), *Ich und die Kaiserin* (1932), *Fanny Elssler* (1937), and many other musical films with Willy Fritsch and Henry Garat. She left Germany for a time and made films for Fox and Columbia in Britain – for example, *Invitation to the Waltz* (1935) – and in America between 1933 and 1935 (*I am Suzanne*). Her last film, *Serenade*, was made in France in 1939.

19b   JEANETTE MACDONALD (b. Philadelphia, 1907; d. 1965)
Publisher: Republic Studios   Photograph: Plaz, Paris

Jeanette MacDonald, an immensely charming star of numerous films, began as a singer on Broadway in the 1920s. Ernst Lubitsch brought her to Hollywood in 1929 for the *Love Parade* with Maurice Chevalier, with whom she also made *One Hour With You* (1932), *Love Me Tonight* (1932) and *The Merry Widow* (1934). Her series of musicals with Nelson Eddy had huge popular success due to her allure and charming singing, and his splendid voice (though not his wooden acting). They made *Naughty Marietta* (1935), *Rose-Marie* (1936), *May Time* (1937), *The Girl of the Golden West* (1938), *New Moon* (1940), *Bitter Sweet* (1940) and *I Married an Angel* (1942). Her other major success was *San Francisco* with Clark Gable in 1936. Her last film was *The Sun Comes Up* in 1949.

19c   GITTA ALPAR (b. Budapest, 1900)
Publisher: 'Ross', Berlin   Autographed

This altitudinous Hungarian soprano began her career with opera and operetta in Hamburg and Berlin (Staatsoper) in the 1920s. She appeared as Sophie in *Der Rosenkavalier* at Covent Garden in 1929, and in the early 'thirties sang the lead in operetta in Vienna, Budapest and London.

She made her first film, *Gitta Entdeckt ihr Herz*, in 1932 with the German actor Gustav Frölich, whom she married on the day of the Berlin première. Her most famous film is *The Dubarry*, made in England in 1936, in which year she also made *Guilty Melody*, directed by Herbert Wilcox, with Anna Neagle. She emigrated to the United States at the beginning of the Second World War and appeared in *The Flame of New Orleans* (1941) directed by René Clair, with Marlene Dietrich and Bruce Cabot.

19d   GRACE MOORE (b. Tennessee, 1901; d. Copenhagen, 1947)
Postmark: 1936, Stockton-on-Tees

The American operatic soprano Grace Moore made her début in a revue called *Hitchy-Koo* (1920) in Boston, which transferred in the same year to the Amsterdam Theatre in New York. She followed this with two seasons of Irving Berlin's *Music Box Revue* in 1923 and 1924.

Grace Moore made her Metropolitan Opera début as Mimi in *La Bohème* in 1928 and followed with Gounod's Juliette and Marguerite, and Massenet's *Manon*. She later added *Louise, L'Amore dei Tre Rè* (Montemezzi) and *Tosca* to her Met repertory. Her Paris début was at the Opéra-Comique as Louise in 1929, and her Covent Garden début in 1935 was as Mimi.

In 1930 she made her first film, *A Lady's Morals*, in which she played Jenny Lind, followed by *New Moon* (1930) with Lawrence Tibbett, her most successful film *One Night of Love* (1934), *Love Me Forever* (1935) and *The King Steps Out* (1940). Her film of Charpentier's opera *Louise* (1939), with George Thill, directed by Abel Gance and made under the composer's supervision, was considered particularly fine.

She wrote her autobiography *You're Only Human Once* in 1946. The following year she was killed in an air crash as her plane was leaving Copenhagen during a European concert tour. The heir to the Swedish throne, Prince Gustav Adolf, was killed in the same crash.

Lilian Harvey

a

JEANETTE MAC DONALD

b

Gitta Alpar

c

GRACE MOORE

d

Theatre
Advertising

20a   LEWIS WALLER AS HENRY V
Publisher: David Allen & Sons, London
Chromotype: Harrow and Belfast   Signed: Arthur Hackin

This is an advertising card for Shakespeare's *Henry V* at the Imperial Theatre in London. The production opened on 21 January 1905 and played for seventy-six performances. The cast included Shiel Barry, Balliol Holloway and Sarah Brooke, and the costumes were by Percy Anderson. Waller had previously played much the same production at the Lyceum in 1900-01, when eighty performances were given.

The Imperial Theatre – which stood where Central Hall, Westminster, now stands – began life as the Royal Aquarium Theatre in 1876, and changed its name to the Imperial in 1879. After a chequered career under managements which included Marie Litton and Lillie Langtry, it was rebuilt and reopened in 1899. It was demolished in 1906 when the site was bought by the Methodists.

For information on Lewis Waller, see **45a**.

20b   *THE TAMING OF THE SHREW*
Publisher: David Allen & Sons   Signed: A. Morrow

Oscar Asche and Lily Brayton's production of Shakespeare's comedy *The Taming of the Shrew* at the Adelphi Theatre in London opened on 29 November 1904 and played for 152 performances. The play was directed by Asche, with costumes by Karl. Asche and his wife Lily Brayton had previously played *The Taming of the Shrew* at the Comedy Theatre in London in 1901, for ten performances.

The Adelphi Theatre in London's Strand began life as the Sans Pareil in 1806, and became the Adelphi in 1819 and the Royal Adelphi in 1829. The present theatre is the fourth built on the site and dates from 1930. It was one of London's most popular theatres in the nineteenth century, and no less than eight Dickens adaptations were given between 1837 and 1845, including *Pickwick*, *Nicholas Nickleby* and *Oliver Twist*. The 1860s saw long runs of *The Colleen Bawn*, *The Octoroon* and *Rip Van Winkle* (with Joseph Jefferson). In 1905, beginning with *The Quaker Girl* (536 performances), the Adelphi became the home of musical comedy. This century has seen performances by Gladys Cooper, Tallulah Bankhead, Evelyn Laye and Cicely Courtneidge, and the Noël Coward revue *Words and Music* in 1932.

20c   *THE DAUGHTERS OF BABYLON*
Publisher: David Allen & Sons, Harrow

This drama in four acts, by the actor Wilson Barrett (1847-1904), starred Wilson Barrett, Constance Collier, Lily Hanbury and Maude Jeffries. It opened on 6 February 1897 and played for seventy-four performances at the Lyric Theatre in London.

This little theatre (994 places) in Shaftesbury Avenue opened in 1888 and was paid for with the profits from the musical comedy *Dorothy*. It was entirely redecorated in 1933.

Previous to *The Daughters of Babylon* the theatre held a long run of Wilson Barrett's *Sign of the Cross*. Réjane and Bernhardt, Forbes-Robertson, Lewis Waller, Martin Harvey and Matheson Lang all appeared here, and in more modern times, Olivier, Richardson, the Lunts and Noël Coward.

20d   *THE GIRL FROM KAY'S*
Publisher: David Allen & Sons Ltd, Belfast   Signed: 'KIN'

George Dance's production of this successful musical comedy opened at the Apollo in London on 15 November 1902, and ran for 433 performances. It transferred to the Comedy Theatre on 14 December 1903, followed by a successful provincial tour and an even greater success in New York.

It starred Willie Edouin as the American millionaire Piggy Hoggenheimer (a rather unsubtle stab at Sir Alfred Rothschild), Ethel Irving in the title role, with Kate Cutler, Letty Lind, Ella Snyder, Kitty Gordon, and Louis Bradfield as the handsome hero. Half of musical London had a hand in the score, including Ivan Caryll, Cecil Cook, Lionel Monckton, Adrian Ross and Paul Rubens.

a

b

c

d

21a   *THE NEVER-NEVER LAND*
             Postmark: August 1904

The four-act drama *The Never-Never Land* was written by Wilson Barrett and first produced at the Variety Theatre in Broughton on 9 April 1902, then at the Grand, Hull, 1 February 1904. It played in London at the King's Theatre, Hammersmith, on 21 March 1904, and, as printed on the reverse of this postcard, at the 'County Theatre, Reading, from Monday 22nd August (1904) for six nights . . . the last play written and produced by the late Wilson Barrett'.

Barrett was one of the great actor-managers of the second half of the nineteenth century; his forte was melodrama. He produced long runs of *The Lights of London*, *The Silver King*, and his own spectacle *The Sign of the Cross*, which made his fortune.

21b   *THE CHARIOT OF BACCHUS* (1905)
             Publisher: Säuberlin et Pfeiffer, Vevey   Signed: E. Biéler

The Fête des Vignerons is a splendid outdoor pageant which takes place in the Place du Marché, in the lovely town of Vevey on the shores of Lac Leman, about once every twenty-five years.

Wine-making has been a way of life for centuries in this part of Switzerland, and this celebration in dance and song is performed by the local populace with only one or two professional actors. The costumes and sets are of great magnificence, and to watch while the sun sinks behind the mountains and night falls is an unforgettable experience.

In existence since the seventeenth century, it was first performed in the Place du Marché in 1799. Since then the grand-scale celebration has been seen in 1819, 1833, 1851, 1865, 1889, 1905, 1927, 1955 and most recently in 1977.

21c   MR ALBERT CHEVALIER'S RECITALS
             Publisher: David Allen & Sons Ltd   Postmark: 17 August 1905

This is an advertisement for the great coster music-hall performer Albert Chevalier at the Town Hall, Burnham, 30 August 1905. The prices were 3 shillings, 2 shillings and 1 shilling, and he was supported by Miss Flossie Behrens, a whistling soloist, as well as two other singers and his pianist.

Chevalier (1861-1923) spent several years in the legitimate theatre before taking to the halls. He wrote many of his own songs and is specially remembered for 'Knocked 'em in the Old Kent Road' and 'My Old Dutch'.

22a   *CHARLEY'S AUNT*
                    Publisher: David Allen & Sons Ltd

Brandon Thomas' evergreen farce *Charley's Aunt* was first performed in 1892 with W. S. Penley as Lord Fancourt Babberley (see **6a**). This advertisement dates from the umpteenth revival, this time at the Savoy Theatre in the Christmas season of 1910. In these performances the masquerading lord was played by Hugh Wakefield.

22b   DORIS KEANE IN *ROMANCE*
                    Publisher: David Allen & Sons Ltd

This card shows an advertisement (from a painting by Charles Buchel) for Edward Sheldon's play *Romance* in three acts with a prologue and epilogue. It was first performed in New York on 10 February 1913, by Maxine Elliot. The first London performances were given at the Duke of York's Theatre, beginning 6 October 1915; it transferred to the Lyric on 15 November, running there for 1047 performances until April 1918. The cast included Owen Nares, Hermann Vezin and Gilda Varesi, but the great triumph was Doris Keane's as the opera singer, Mme Cavallini, who has the memorable line: 'Go make de love to dose bee-eautiful Amer'can ladies vit' de long nose an' de neck full of beetle bones'! Also this gem: 'Love is de 'unger for anoder's flesh – a deep down t'irst to dreenk anoder's blood – love is a beast dat feed all t'rough de night an' vhen de morning come – love dies!' Doris Keane must have been some actress!

22c   FOLIES-BERGÈRE
                    Publisher: Philipp & Kramer, Vienna
                    Signed: Walter Hampl

The Théâtre des Folies-Bergère was inaugurated on 2 May 1869 and was the first of the many music halls in Paris. Most of the great European stars played there – Anna Judic, La Belle Otéro, Liane de Pougy, Lina Cavalieri, La Tortojada, Gaby Delys, Cléo de Mérode, Maurice Chevalier, Mistinguett, Yvonne Printemps, Josephine Baker, Fernandel, Raimu and countless others.

   This advertisement is number 5 in the series XXX, 'Les Cafés Chantants', printed in 1900 for the Paris World Fair.

22d   *THE MAID OF THE MOUNTAINS*
                    Publisher: David Allen & Sons

The advertisement pictures Josie Collins as Teresa in Oscar Asche's production of *The Maid of the Mountains* which opened at Daly's on 10 February 1917 and totalled 1353 performances in this initial run – closing on 2 April 1920. It had its première in Manchester prior to the London run, on 23 December 1916. This charming musical play in three acts has music by Harold Frazer-Simpson with added numbers by J. W. Tate. The sets were by Joseph Harker, costumes by Comelli, and choreography by Espinoza.

a

From a Painting by Charles Buchel.

b

c

d

Opera   **23a**   LINA CAVALIERI (b. Viterbo, 1874; d. Florence, 1944)
Photograph: Reutlinger, Paris

Reared on the streets and orphaned at fifteen, the exquisitely beautiful Lina Cavalieri learned to fight for what she wanted. She ran away from a convent orphanage and joined a theatrical troupe touring the Italian provinces. She made her way to Vienna and Paris, singing in the café-concerts, and by the time she was twenty sported valuable trophies from half the crowned heads of Europe, or anyone rich enough for her.

Lina Cavalieri's amorous proclivities did not hinder her career. She studied with Mariani-Masi, Ponchielli's first Gioconda, and made her début in Lisbon as Nedda in *I Pagliacci* in 1900. Unsuccessful at first, she went on to sing Manon, Thaïs, Violetta, Tosca, Fedora and many other roles, in Europe, Russia and America. She appeared in all the great opera houses and although her voice was less than first-class, she was the greatest beauty in the world.

Her love life always made good copy – she vowed that she had received 840 proposals of marriage, though she only accepted four. Even Mussolini was mentioned among her lovers. Although this spoilt beauty's emeralds were said to be the size of pigeon eggs, she was a generous woman. She campaigned for orphans, she donned khaki and entertained the French troops at the front in the First World War, and became a nurse during the Second. She died in an air raid just outside Florence in 1944.

23b   EMMA CALVE (b. 1858; d.1942) as Ophélie
Photograph: Reutlinger   Postmark: 30 December 1906

Emma Calvé was a remarkably well-schooled French soprano and a formidable actress who had a long and honourable career. Although she made her début in Brussels in 1882, her first ten years were only moderately successful.

The great influences on Emma Calvé were Victor Maurel, Rosine Laborde and Eleanora Duse – she followed the latter on her tours unbeknown to the great actress. Her voice was a soprano of some substance, to which she added several falsetto notes which took her up to a high E. During her career she sang an enormous variety of parts, including Lucia, Amina, Ophélie, both Salomé and Hérodiade (in Massenet's opera), Santuzza and Carmen. She was considered the greatest Carmen of her day and sang it in all the great opera houses. For Massenet she created the roles of Anita in *La Navarraise* and Sapho.

She was a great favourite at Covent Garden and the Metropolitan Opera, and continued on the stage until 1910.

23c   MIZZI GÜNTHER (b. 1879; d. 1961) as Princess Photini in *Das Fürstenkind*
Photograph: L. Gutmann, Vienna

Mizzi Günther was the queen of operetta in Vienna in the first years of this century. She created the star roles in seven operettas of Franz Lehár: *Der Rastelbinder* (1902), *Die Göttergatte* (1904), *The Merry Widow* (1905), *Das Fürstenkind* (1909), *Eva* (1911), *Die Ideale Gattin* (1913) and *Endlich Allein* (1914). The most famous was the everlasting *Merry Widow* which had its first performance in the Theater an der Wien, conducted by the composer, on 30 December 1905, and has ever since been performed constantly – everywhere. The directors of the theatre had so little faith in the piece that Mizzi Günther was obliged to pay for her own glamorous costumes. During her career she sang more than 1500 times in performances of Lehár, 700 of which were as the Merry Widow herself.

23d   EMMA EAMES (b. 1865; d. 1952)
Publisher: Breitkopf & Härtel, New York
Photograph: Aimé Dupont

The American soprano Emma Eames was born in Shanghai and began her studies in Boston. She went to Paris and studied with Marchesi whom she called the Prussian drill-master, and came to loggerheads with Melba whom she would detest to the end of her life. Both singers were coached by Gounod as Juliette, and the composer facilitated Eames' début in the role at the Opéra in 1889. Each of the two women thought she was his ideal Juliette.

Eames made her Covent Garden and Metropolitan Opera débuts as Juliette in 1891, and spent most of her career in these two houses. She excelled as Desdemona, Marguerite, the Countess in *Figaro*, Eva, Elsa, Elisabeth and Sieglinde. Her middle voice was of an especially rich timbre.

a

b

c

d

24a   LEO SLEZAK (b. 1873; d. 1946) as Canio in Leoncavallo's
               I Pagliacci
               Publisher: Iris Verlag, Vienna   Photograph: Residenz

The Austrian tenor Leo Slezak made his début in Brno, Czechoslovakia, in 1896 as Lohengrin. He was 6 feet 2 inches tall, with a splendid dramatic voice, and excelled as Wagner's heroes. He also sang *Les Huguenots* and *Le Prophète* of Meyerbeer, Tamino and Belmonte of Mozart, Radames, Manrico and Otello of Verdi, all with success in the great theatres of Berlin, London, New York and Vienna (to which he was faithful for thirty-three years).

Toward the end of his life Leo Slezak made films and wrote several volumes of reminiscences.

24b   ENRICO CARUSO (b. 1873; d. 1921) as Raoul in *Les Huguenots*
               Publisher: J. Beagles & Co., London
               Photograph: Ellis & Walery   c. 1906 (in pen on verso)

Throughout his entire career Caruso sang the role of Raoul (or 'Raul' as he sang it in an Italian translation) about eighteen times. In 1896, the second year of his career, he sang it for the first time in the Teatro Bellini in Naples, not singing it again until 1905, at the Metropolitan Opera. His partners on this latter occasion were Sembrich, Nordica, Journet and Plançon. In the same year he sang three performances in Covent Garden with Destinn, Kurz, Whitehill, Scotti and Journet. On 8 June in the same season, with substantially the same cast, he sang the fourth act at Buckingham Palace in a gala honouring the King and Queen of Spain. He revived it at the Metropolitan Opera, New York, in 1912 for five performances, with Destinn, Hempel, Alten, Scotti, Rothier and Didur, and sang it the following year on tour with the Metropolitan in Philadelphia. It was revived once again at the Met for three performances in 1914. He recorded the first-act aria twice, once with piano in 1905 and with orchestra in 1909.

24c   JOHN McCORMACK (b. Athlone, 1884; d. 1945)
               Publisher: Breitkopf & Härtel
               Photograph: Dover Studios, London

The Irish tenor John McCormack made his début in Savona under the name of Giovanni Foli in Mascagni's *L'Amico Fritz* in 1906. He had a true Irish tenor of great sweetness and considerable technique. Reverting to his own name, he sang in the opera houses of Europe and America (and in Australia), often with Melba and Tetrazzini, in *La Bohème, La Traviata, Don Giovanni, Lucia, Faust, Martha, Tosca* and *Cavalleria. Bohème* he sang most of all – with eighteen different sopranos, his favourite being Lucrezia Bori.

John McCormack made extensive concert tours as far as China and Japan, and made an enormous number of recordings. Although many of the titles are rather trifling, his recording of 'Il mio tesoro' from *Don Giovanni* is legendary. He made a fortune, much of which he gave to the Catholic Church which rewarded him with the title of Count.

24d   LAURITZ MELCHIOR (b. 1890; d. 1973) as Otello
               Postmark: 23 October 1928, Hamburg

The leading Wagnerian tenor of his time, Lauritz Melchior began as a baritone in his own native Denmark in 1913. In 1918 he made a second début, in Copenhagen (as Tannhäuser), and from then onward became the leading German tenor at Covent Garden, Bayreuth and the Metropolitan Opera, where he sang frequently with Kirsten Flagstad. He made his last appearance at this latter house aged sixty, as Lohengrin.

A huge man with incredible stamina, he made a few Hollywood films in the 'forties and 'fifties which are fairly dreadful.

On the verso of this postcard his wife Maria writes to Professor Kittel in Bayreuth (her husband is a guest at the Berlin Staatsoper): 'In November is the first Tristan! January 1927 we are in Spain for 6 performances of Tristan and Tannhäuser in Barcelona. February to April in New York Metropolitan, then immediately in London-Covent Garden until the end of May'.

Foto:RESIDENZ

Leo Slezak

a

705 D
J. BEAGLES & Co.
E.C.

CARUSO

ELLIS & WALERY.

b

John Mc Cormack

162.

Copyright by Dover Street Studios.

c

Melchior
als „Othello"

Lauritz Melchior.

d

25a MAURICE RENAUD (b. Bordeaux, 1861; d. Paris, 1933) as
Don Giovanni
Publisher:F. C. et Cie   Photograph: Paul Berger

Maurice Renaud was the greatest French baritone of his day and an actor of considerable strength. He sang mainly in Paris, London, Brussels and New York, and although much of his repertory was French he excelled as Don Giovanni, Scarpia, Wolfram and Beckmesser. His characterisation of Thomas' Hamlet, Saint-Säen's Henry VIII, and Mephistopheles in Berlioz' *The Damnation of Faust* were landmarks in operatic history.

His Gallic bel canto-verismo style was perhaps best suited to Massenet. He created the role of Boniface in *Le Jongleur de Notre-Dame* (1902) and the Philosopher in *Chérubin* (1905), but is best remembered for his stunning portrayals of Herod in *Hérodiade* and Athanaël in *Thaïs*.

25b JOHN FORSELL (b. Stockholm, 1868; d. Stockholm, 1941) as
John the Baptist in Richard Strauss' *Salomé*
Publisher: Paul Heckscher

Sweden's greatest baritone, John Forsell, obviously preferred to stay at home. His operatic repertoire included over sixty roles and he sang all these in the Royal Theatre in Stockholm in the years 1896-1917. He sang 135 performances of Eugene Onegin, 122 of Don Giovanni, 107 of Count Almaviva in *Figaro*, 94 of the Flying Dutchman, 65 of Alfonso in *La Favorita*, 57 of Scarpia, 46 of William Tell and multi-performances of his other roles. He sang a fair amount in major houses in north Germany, but only once at Covent Garden – *Don Giovanni* in 1909.

John Forsell was praised for the beauty of his voice, security of technique and the liveliness of his acting. In the 1909-10 season he was heard at the Metropolitan Opera in New York as Telramund, Rossini's Figaro, Germont, and Prince Yeletzky in *The Queen of Spades* (conducted by Gustav Mahler), as well as in seven operatic concerts.

He was made Intendant of the Royal Opera in Stockholm in 1924, but temporarily left this duty to sing Don Giovanni at the Salzburg Festival in 1930.

25c MARIO SAMMARCO (b. Palermo, 1873; d. Milan, 1930)
Autographed: 'Buenos-Ayres 1904'

The career of the Sicilian baritone Mario Sammarco covered over thirty years, during which he sang in the great theatres of Italy, Great Britain, Russia, South America and the United States (excepting the Metropolitan Opera).

He is important historically as he created two great verismo roles: Gérard in *Andrea Chénier* at La Scala in 1896, and Cascart in Leoncavallo's *Zazà* in 1900 at the Teatro Lirico in Milan. The verismo style suited his voice best and he was particularly praised as Scarpia and Tonio.

His message on the postcard reads: 'Excuse the delay'.

25d VICTOR MAUREL (b. Marseilles, 1848; d. New York, 1923) as
Don Giovanni
Rotary Photographic Series   Autographed and dated 1904

A great genius of French theatre, Victor Maurel has his place in history as the creator of Tonio in *I Pagliacci* for Leoncavallo (1892), and Iago (1887) and Falstaff (1893) for Verdi.

A long distinguished career took him to the great theatres of the world. He made his début in 1867 in Rossini's *Guillaume Tell*, and encompassed in his lifetime a great deal of the baritone repertoire. He excelled in Wagner and Verdi, and his Don Giovanni was considered extremely elegant.

RENAUD
de l'Opéra.

a

b

Baritono Sammarco

c

VICTOR MAUREL

d

26a   DMITRI SMIRNOV (b. 1881; d. 1944) as the Duke in *Rigoletto*
               Photograph: K. A. Fischer, Moscow and St Petersburg

The Russian tenor Dmitri Smirnov made his début at the Imperial Theatre in 1904. He came to Paris with Diaghilev in 1908 and introduced *Boris Godunov* to the West in the company of Chaliapin. He sang in *La Traviata* with Selma Kurz in the same season, and with Elvira de Hidalgo, Ruffo and Chaliapin in *Il Barbiere di Siviglia*. The following year *Rusalka* was introduced, when he again sang with Chaliapin, and he also appeared with Frieda Hempel in *Rigoletto*. The same year he sang in *Mefistofele* (Boito) with Chaliapin in Monte Carlo.

Smirnov made his début at the Metropolitan Opera in *Rigoletto* in 1910 with his compatriot, Lydia Lipkowska, and then sang Roméo with Geraldine Farrar; he stayed there for two seasons.

He was unpopular in Russia after the Revolution as he chose to sing mainly in the West. In 1926 he was heard in recital in New York. He had an elegant lyric voice with enormous breath control, and phrased with much subtlety.

26b   TITTA RUFFO (b. Pisa, 1877; d. Florence, 1953) in *Hamlet* by
               Ambroise Thomas
               Autographed and inscribed with the music for the words 'To be, or
               not to be?'; dated 2.9.1910, Buenos Aires

One of the truly great voices of all time, the baritone Titta Ruffo was blessed by Nature with a huge, large-ranging ringing sound which allowed him to dominate all the great theatres.

Hamlet was his *'cheval de bataille'*; he sang it for the first time in Lisbon in 1907, then in Milan, Warsaw, Madrid, Valencia, Barcelona, Buenos Aires, Rome, Naples, Montevideo, São Paolo, Rio de Janiero, Paris, Budapest, New York, Chicago, Philadelphia, Florence, Genoa, Mexico City, Havana, Santiago, San Juan, Caracas, Bogotà, Pisa, Valparaiso, Cannes, and made his farewell to the role in Nice with most of Acts 2 and 3 in 1934. Over the years he sang the same role many times in the same city, and in all sang close to 150 performances of the opera.

His other great roles were Tonio in *I Pagliacci*, *Rigoletto*, Don Carlos in *Ernani*, Gérard in *Andrea Chénier*, Barnaba in *La Gioconda*, Figaro and Scarpia.

26c   FEODOR CHALIAPIN (b. Kazan, 1873; d. Paris, 1938) as
               Mephistopheles in Gounod's *Faust*

Supreme as a singer and an actor, the influence of the gigantic Russian bass, Chaliapin, is felt to this day. From his beginnings as a poor peasant in Russia, he rose to the very top of his profession internationally. He excelled in Russian roles – Boris Godunov, the Miller in Dargomyzhsky's *Rusalka*, Susanin in Glinka's *A Life for the Tsar*, Dosifey in Mussorgsky's *Knovanshchina*, Ivan the Terrible in Rimsky-Korsakov's *The Maid of Pskov*, and Salieri in Rimsky-Korsakov's *Mozart and Salieri*.

Chaliapin produced a new excitement in several repertory roles – the Mephistopheles of Gounod and Boito, Massenet's Don Quichotte, Rossini's Basilio and Mozart's Leoporello.

26d   LEONID SOBINOV (b. 1872; d. 1934) as Lensky in *Eugene
               Onegin*

The Russian tenor Leonid Sobinov began his career at the very end of the nineteenth century in a rather obscure and totally forgotten Russian opera, but by 1902 he was already singing *Faust*, the Duke in *Rigoletto* and Lensky in *Eugene Onegin* at the Maryinsky in St Petersburg. In 1904, and in subsequent seasons, he sang at La Scala, Milan, in *Fra Diavolo*, *Don Pasquale*, *La Traviata*, *Falstaff*, *Manon* and *Werther*. From 1907 onward he sang mainly in Russia and remained there after the Revolution, singing his repertory of lyric roles including Gérald in *Lakmé*, Nadir in *The Pearl Fishers*, Wilhelm in *Mignon* and Gluck's *Orfeo*. He was a true exponent of bel canto.

530.   Д. А. СМИРНОВЪ. (Оп. «Риголетто»)
Соб. фотогр. и худ. фотот. К. А. Фишеръ, Москва—С.-Петербургъ.   **a**

Titta Ruffo   **b**

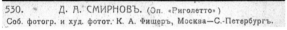

Ф. ШАЛЯПИНЪ „МЕФИСТОФЕЛЬ" въ оперъ „ФАУСТЪ".   **c**

2914.   Л. В. СОБИНОВЪ. (Оп. „Евгеній Онѣгинъ").
Соб. изд. фотогр. и худож. фотот. К. Фишеръ, Москва—С.-Петербургъ.   **d**

27a   HARICLÉA DARCLÉE (b. Bucharest, 1860; d. Bucharest, 1939)

Haricléa Darclée's place in history is secure as Puccini's first Tosca, created in Rome in 1900. After studying in her native Roumania, she went to Paris and worked with the great baritone, Jean-Baptiste Faure. She made her début at the Opéra as Marguérite in *Faust* in 1888, and the following year substituted for Patti in *Roméo et Juliette*. She created the roles of La Wally (Catalani), Iris (Mascagni) and Luisa in *I Rantzau* (Mascagni) and was the first La Scala Elisabeth in Wagner's *Tannhäuser* in 1894. She was a well-schooled soprano, at home with the romantic heroines of Donizetti and Verdi before singing to a large extent in the verismo school. She retired from the stage in 1918 with a performance of Carmen in Florence.

27b   CLARA BUTT (b. 1873; d. 1936)
                 Rotary Photographic Series
                 Photograph: Fellows Wilson, Kensington   Hand-coloured

The contralto of Clara Butt was of commensurate size and beauty to her handsome features and height of 6 feet 2 inches. In her prime she had a huge range from the low bass E of her remarkable chest voice to a clarion high B flat, and it was said that hers was the greatest contralto since Alboni.

Clara Butt's only operatic role was Gluck's Orpheus, which she sang at Covent Garden. Elgar wrote his *Sea Pictures* for her, and she sang them for the first time at the Norwich Festival of 1899. Apart from the English festivals, she toured the world giving recitals with her handsome baritone husband, Kennerley Rumford, often following Melba's advice on her forthcoming Australian tour to 'sing 'em muck'.

She was created a Dame of the British Empire in 1920 in recognition of her charitable work during the war.

27c   ERNESTINE SCHUMANN-HEINK (b. near Prague, 1861;
                 d. Hollywood, 1936)
                 Publisher: The Rose Company, Philadelphia, 1907
                 Hand-coloured

The Bohemian-born contralto (and American citizen from 1905) Ernestine Schumann-Heink was one of the most beloved singers of all time. She sang mainly in the Wagnerian repertoire at Covent Garden, Bayreuth, and the Metropolitan Opera. She made her début aged fifteen singing Beethoven's Ninth Symphony (the 'Choral') and made her farewell to the operatic stage singing Erda at the Metropolitan Opera, aged seventy. She continued to sing in concerts – concluding a career lasting sixty years.

She sang Fidès in Meyerbeer's *Le Prophète* with resounding success, and created Clytemnestra in Richard Strauss' *Elektra* in 1909. It is worth mentioning that she found time for three husbands and seven children.

Hariclée Darclée
nell'Opera "Tosca"

a

180 C ROTARY PHOTO. E.C.   MISS CLARA BUTT.   PHOTO. FELLOWS WILLSON. 57 BEDFORD GDNS. KENSINGTON.

b

"Waltraute" in "Gotterdammerung"   "Erda" in "Rheingold and Siegfried"

c

28a   SYBIL SANDERSON (b. Sacramento, 1865; d. Paris, 1903) as
                 Leila in Bizet's *Les Pêcheurs de Perles*
                 Publisher: Vanderauwera, Brussels and Paris
                 Photograph: Dupont

Massenet in his forties first heard the three octaves of Sybil Sanderson and was completely besotted by her beguiling person as well as her charming voice. He arranged for her to sing his Manon in the Hague, then wrote *Esclarmonde* for her during the Paris Exhibition (Opéra-Comique, 1889) and later *Thaïs* (Opéra-Comique, 1894). The young American soprano was very much to Parisian taste – she sang Esclarmonde 101 times in nine months; successes elsewhere, especially in her own country, were fewer.

She married a wealthy Cuban in 1897 and became the châtelaine of the Castle of Chenonceaux. After her husband's death in 1899 she returned to the stage, but died very young of pneumonia, aged thirty-eight.

Massenet never forgot her and would not allow a revival of *Esclarmonde*, which he loved above all his operas, during his lifetime.

28b   GERALDINE FARRAR (b. 1882; d. 1967) as Violetta in
                 La Traviata, 1905

The daughter of an American baseball player, Geraldine Farrar was highly gifted by Nature – both vocally and physically. She studied in Germany with Lilli Lehmann and made her début in Berlin in 1901 as Marguérite, with Karl Muck conducting. She sang with enormous success there and in Paris and Monte Carlo for several years, creating the role of Amica for Mascagni in 1905 at Monte Carlo. Her Metropolitan Opera début was as Juliette for the opening night of the 1906-07 season. She added *Butterfly* to her repertoire, a role she would perform ninety-five times in her sixteen seasons there.

Geraldine Farrar never completely mastered her vocal technique, relying very much on her beauty and overt dramatic talent. However, she remained a firm favourite with the public and had enormous successes with Leoncavallo's Zaza, Humperdinck's Goose Girl, Manon, Charlotte, Mimi, Carmen and many other roles. She created Puccini's *Suor Angelica*, which had its première at the Metropolitan Opera in 1918.

Deciding to leave the stage in 1922, she went to Hollywood and made very successful silent films, including *Carmen* and *The World and Its Women*, with her husband (for a short time only) Lou Tellegen.

28c   EMMY DESTINN (b. Prague, 1878; d. Budweis, 1930) as
                 Mignon
                 Publisher: Hermann Leiser, Berlin
                 Photograph: Atelier Victoria, Berlin

The Czech soprano Emmy Destinn made her début in Dresden as Santuzza in 1897, and then became a member of the Berlin Opera for ten years. She made her Covent Garden début in 1905 as Madame Butterfly and her Met début in 1908 as Aida. These two roles were her greatest interpretations, and in them she was idolised by the public on both sides of the Atlantic. Puccini wrote the role of Minnie in *La Fanciulla del West* for her; she created this at the Metropolitan Opera in 1910 with Caruso. Her other famous roles included La Gioconda, Pamina, Valentine in *Les Huguenots*, Leonora in *Trovatore*, Nedda, Eva, Elsa and Elisabeth, Senta and Mařenka in *The Bartered Bride*.

28d   FRANCES ALDA (b. Christchurch, 1883; d. Vienna, 1952) as
                 La Wally
                 Publisher: Breitkopf & Härtel, New York
                 Photograph: Aimé Dupont

The Australian soprano Frances Alda was born Frances Davies in New Zealand. Brought up in Australia, she studied with Mathilde Marchesi in Paris, married the director of the Metropolitan Opera, Giulio Gatti-Casazza, and sang at the Met from 1908 until her retirement in 1930. She was one of the more colourful personalities on the operatic scene of her day, and her backstage interference in casting, allied with her feuds with Melba and others, always made good copy.

She was well-born operatically speaking – her grandmother was Fanny Simonsen, prima donna of the Simonsen Opera Company in Australia, and her mother was soprano Frances Saville who sang at the Met, Covent Garden and Vienna. Alda herself sang at La Scala, Covent Garden, L'Opéra-Comique, the Teatro Colón and in Montevideo, where her grandmother had sung before her. She created the roles of Madame Chrysanthème (Messager) and Victor Herbert's Madeleine. Her best roles were the two Manons, Mimi, Marguérite in *Faust*, and Desdemona. She was said to display more temperament off-stage than on.

SYBIL SANDERSON (DANS LES PÊCHEURS DE PERLES)

a

Geraldine Farrar
i. Traviata

b

Emmy Destinn
a „Mignon",

Photo Atelier Victoria, Berlin W.

Hermann Leiser

c

Frances Alda
La Wally

"Copyright by Aimé Dupont"

d

29a   ANTONIA NEZHDANOVA (b. 1873; d. 1950)
                 Hand-coloured

The great Russian coloratura soprano made her début in Moscow (1902) in Glinka's *A Life for the Tsar* and was at once engaged by the Bolshoi. Throughout the thirty years of her career she sang most of the high repertoire: Gilda, Lakmé, Juliette, Frau Fluth in *The Merry Wives of Windsor*, The Queen of the Night, Queen Marguerite in *Les Huguenots*, Ophélie, Zerlina in *Fra Diavolo*, in addition to more dramatic roles such as Desdemona and Tosca as well as the Russian repertoire.

   Antonia Nezhdanova confined her career to Russia, with the exception of the 1912 season at Monte Carlo and Paris, when she sang Gilda in *Rigoletto* with Caruso and Ruffo.

29b   MARIA SLAVINA (b. 1858; d. ?) as Amneris in *Aida*
                 Hand-coloured

The Russian mezzo-soprano-contralto, Maria Slavina, was one of the major voices of her day. In St Petersburg she created the roles of Anna in Rimsky-Korsakov's *May Night* in 1880, Konchakovna in Borodin's *Prince Igor* and the old Countess in Tchaikovsky's *Queen of Spades*, both in 1890, and Clytemnestra in Taneyev's *Oresteia* in 1895. She sang the Wagner contralto roles as well as Fidès in *Le Prophète*, Amneris and Carmen. She left Russia at the time of the Revolution.

29c   MARGARETHE SIEMS (b. 1879; d. 1952)
                 Publisher: Gustav Schmidt, Dresden, 1909

The German soprano Margarethe Siems must be counted as one of the most extraordinary singers of all time, on account of her wildly diverse repertoire performed with an amazing technique.

   She was a pupil of Aglaia Orgeni, the Hungarian soprano who was a pupil of Pauline Viardot. She made her operatic career largely in Dresden, but with forays to London, St Petersburg and Milan. For Richard Strauss she created Chrysothemis (1909) and the Marschallin (1911), both in Dresden, and the first and very high version of Zerbinetta in *Ariadne auf Naxos* (1912) in Stuttgart. She also sang the Queen of the Night, Lucia, Philine and Gilda, as well as Aida and Madama Butterfly.

29d   NATALIA ERMOLENKO (b. 1881; d. ?) as Masha in
                 Nápravník's *Dubrovsky*, 1895
                 Photograph: K. Fischer, Moscow   Hand-coloured

One of the greatest Russian dramatic sopranos, Natalia Ermolenko's career was spent mainly in St Petersburg and Moscow. She sang Marina in *Boris Godunov* during Diaghilev's 1908 Paris season, and her ample voice and regal bearing were highly praised.

   Natalia Ermolenko's repertoire included Norma, Brünnhilde, Valentine in *Les Huguenots*, Margherita in *Mefistofele*, and Violetta, along with the Russian roles of Lisa in *The Queen of Spades* and Jaroslavna in *Prince Igor*. After she married the tenor David Yuzhin, she sang as Ermolenko-Yuzhina. She left Russia some years after the Revolution and disappeared from sight.

Negdanowa „Lakmé"

a

Славина   0296

b

Margarete Siems

c

3039. Н. С. ЕРМОЛЕНКО-ЮЖИНА (Оп. „Дубровскій").

Ermolenko-Jugina sopran

d

30a   CARMEN, Act IV
                    Publisher: Raphael Tuck et Fils, Paris   Hand-coloured
                    Postmark: 7 April 1903

Series of scenes from all the popular operas were photographed – often with photographic models rather than singers. They are frequently quaint and amusing in a manner not quite intended.

30b   THE MERRY WIDOW, Act II
                    Photograph: Schmoll, Berlin   Hand-coloured

This looks like the original Widow and Danilo, Mizzi Günther and Louis Treumann, which would date the card 1905 or 1906.

30c   FAUST, Act III
                    Hand-coloured

A French card showing the Garden Scene in Gounod's *Faust*, much as it may have looked in a turn-of-the-century performance.

30d   ROMÉO ET JULIETTE, Act V
                    Photograph: Dix, Paris   Hand-coloured

These two have posed themselves decoratively for the Tomb Scene in Gounod's *Roméo et Juliette*.

Carmen

Jamais Carmen ne cédera
Libre elle est née et libre elle mourra.

a

Hanna ich liebe dich"
„na endlich"

b

Mephistopheles à Faust :
Vous voyez qu'elle a fait bon accueil aux bijoux.

5

c

Juliette :
O joie infinie et suprême
De mourir avec toi !....Viens ..un baiser..je t'aime
Seigneur ! seigneur ! pardonnez-nous.

10

d

Theatre
Composers

31a   GIACOMO PUCCINI (b. 1858; d. 1924)
              Photograph: Alterocca Terni, circa 1900

The composer of *La Bohème, Tosca, Madama Butterfly*, et al. about the age of forty.

31b   RICHARD STRAUSS (b. 1864; d. 1949)
              Publisher: Hermann Leiser, Berlin

Richard Strauss in 1894, the year in which his first opera, *Guntram*, had its première at the Court Theatre in Weimar (10 May 1894). Pauline de Alma, who was to become his wife, sang the leading soprano role.

31c   GIUSEPPE VERDI (b. 1813; d. 1901)

A card commemorating the death of Verdi on 27 January 1901. It is postmarked 29 February 1901, Napoli.

GIACOMO PUCCINI

1727 - Alterocca Terni

a

Richard Strauss
(1894)

Verl. Herm. Leiser, Berlin-Wilm.

8707

b

c

32a   RICHARD WAGNER (b. 1813; d. 1883)
             Postmark: 28 March 1901, Neufchateau

The Wagner villa Triebschen, outside Lucerne, Switzerland, is now a museum devoted to Wagner. A plaque on the house declares: 'In this house Richard Wagner lived from April 1866 until April 1872. Here he finished composing *Die Meistersinger, Siegfried, Götterdämmerung, Beethoven* (an article published, 2nd December 1870), *Kaisermarsch, Siegfried-Idyll*'.

32b   GRÜSS AUS BAYREUTH
             Publisher: F. Förster   Postmark: 27 July 1897, Bayreuth

This is the second part of a series of postcards sent by the Wagnerian conductor, Karl Richter, to his daughter Mathilde, about a musical evening at Wahnfried, the Wagner home. He wrote that he greatly enjoyed himself in spite of all the aristocratic visitors, and that he and the sister-in-law of Ellen Gulbranson (the Wagnerian soprano) made short work of the buffet supper.

The vignettes show the interior and exterior of the Wagner theatre in Bayreuth, and the Wagnerian tenor Alois Burgstaller as Siegfried – he was the first American Parsifal at the Metropolitan Opera in 1903. In the same season he sang both Siegmund and Siegfried, as well as Erik in *The Flying Dutchman*. He sang at the Met every season until 1909.

32c   ISOLDE
             Lithograph: Kunstanstalt Heinr. & Aug. Brüning Hanau (Richard
             Wagner Series No. 1)   Postmark: 24 December 1889, Vienna

This chromolithograph depicts Rosa Sucher (1849-1927) as Isolde in Wagner's *Tristan und Isolde*. She was famous as a Wagnerian soprano and sang at Bayreuth every year from 1886 to 1899. She sang Isolde at the Metropolitan Opera in 1895.

a

b

c

Drama   33a   ELLEN TERRY (b. 1847; d. 1928)
                                 Publisher: J. Beagles & Co., London
                                 Photograph: H. S. Mendelssohn
                                 Postmark: 14 August 1907, Middlesex

England's most beloved actress, Ellen Terry, was born into a family of actors – her parents, three sisters and brother, as well as numerous descendants, were all members of the profession. Her great partnership with Henry Irving lasted from 1878 until 1902; after his death she continued to act until 1925, in which year she was created Dame Grand Cross of the British Empire at the age of seventy-eight.

One of the more extraordinary events in Ellen Terry's career was the matinee Benefit Jubilee given in 1906 at Drury Lane. Practically every great name in British theatre was there to honour her and many foreign stars besides. W. S. Gilbert directed and appeared in his own *Trial by Jury* with Rutland Barrington, Courtice Pounds, Henry Lytton and Walter Passmore; among the bridesmaids were no less than Billie Burke, Zena Dare, Gabrielle Ray and Gertie Millar, while Sir Arthur Conan Doyle was a member of the Jury.

There was a series of tableaux vivants in which appeared Lillie Langtry, Constance Collier, the Vanbrugh sisters, Lilian Braithwaite, Edna May and dozens more. Ellen Terry herself played her famous role of Beatrice in Act 1 of *Much Ado About Nothing* with Forbes-Robertson, Beerbohm-Tree, Hermann Vezin, Oscar Asche, and twenty-two members of her family – including her grandchildren – in various parts. Caruso sang accompanied by Tosti. Adeline Genée danced. Mrs Patrick Campbell recited. At the end of the six-hour programme, Ellen Terry appeared on stage surrounded by the whole cast as well as Réjane, Jane Hading and Eleanora Duse, who had come from Florence especially. Ellen spoke: 'I will not say goodbye...'

              33b   ELLEN TERRY and JAMES CAREW in *Henry of Lancaster*
                                 Publisher: J. Beagles   Photograph: Ellis & Walery

When Ellen Terry was fifty-nine and playing in Shaw's *Captain Brassbound's Conversion*, which he wrote for her, the cast included a young American actor of thirty-six, James Carew (1875-1938). Ellen Terry elevated him to her leading man on her American tour the following year (1907) and married him secretly in Pittsburg. The marriage lasted a short time only, due in part to the insane resentment of her daughter, Edy.

They are pictured here in Gladys Unger's romantic drama *Henry of Lancaster*, which they played early in 1908 on tour, beginning at the Theatre Royal, Nottingham, on 28 February.

              33c   ELEONORA DUSE (b. Vigevano, 1859; d. Pittsburg, 1924) in
                                 Francesca da Rimini
                                 Photograph: Sciutto   Autographed (in her favourite purple ink)

The great Italian tragedian, Eleonora Duse, is pictured here as Francesca in Gabriele d'Annunzio's five-act tragedy, *Francesca da Rimini* (Ermete Zacconi was Paolo).

Duse played the first performance at the Teatro Costanzi, Rome, in December 1901, the work directed and supervised in all departments by her lover, d'Annunzio, who allowed her to pay the astronomic costs. This was a tempestuous, not to say catastrophic relationship; nevertheless he dedicated the play 'To the divine Eleonora Duse'. The press, on the day after the première, wrote of 'her divine caressing voice with her own spiritual tone that illumines and blesses the listener'.

              33d   ELEONORA DUSE in *La Città Morta*

This postcard shows Eleonora Duse as the blind Anna, in Act 1 of d'Annunzio's tragedy, *La Città Morta*, which played in Milan with Ermete Zacconi in 1901.

The drama had been first promised to Duse, but d'Annunzio then underhandedly offered it to Sarah Bernhardt who played it in a French translation in Paris in 1898. Duse originally dressed Anna in white but soon changed her mind and had the costumes remade in black. She kept the play in her repertoire right up until her last American tours.

537 W MATT.
G 537 W GLOSSY.   MISS ELLEN TERRY.   J. BEAGLES & CO.

H.S.Mendelssohn.

a

1850
BEAGLES' POSTCARDS   MISS ELLEN TERRY. & MR. JAMES CAREW   ELLIS & WALERY
COPYRIGHT.
"HENRY OF LANCASTER"

b

ELEONORA DUSE

573

c

7402

Eleonora Duse.

d

34a   JOHN MARTIN HARVEY (b. 1863; d. 1944) as Louis dei
Franchi in *The Corsican Brothers*, 1907
Publisher: J. Beagles & Co. Ltd   Photograph: Ellis & Walery

The British actor-manager Martin Harvey first played a secondary role in Dion Boucicault's 1852 adaptation of Dumas' *Les Frères Corses* at the Lyceum, with Henry Irving playing the two brothers, in 1891. He produced his own version at the Theatre Royal, Birmingham, and transferred it to London's Adelphi in 1907.

A true romantic actor, he is remembered for his performances of Sydney Carton in *The Only Way*, his Pelléas which he played to Mrs Patrick Campbell's Mélisande, as well as countless melodramas such as *Ib and Little Christina*, *The Cigarette Maker's Romance*, *The Breed of the Treshams*, *Boy O'Carroll* and many others. His Hamlet and Richard III were considered very fine, as was his Oedipus Rex. In 1921 he received a knighthood for his services to the theatre.

34b   MATHESON LANG (b. Montreal, 1879; d. 1948) as Dick
Dudgeon in *The Devil's Disciple*
Rotary Photo   Photograph: Ellis & Walery
Hand-coloured

Early in his career (before his London triumphs) the exceedingly handsome Matheson Lang toured with Lillie Langtry and Ellen Terry. He first played Dick Dudgeon in George Bernard Shaw's *The Devil's Disciple* at the Savoy in 1907, just after his outstanding success in *The Christian* at the Lyceum. It was here also that he gave his splendid performances of Hamlet and Romeo. (He would later inaugurate the Shakespeare productions in 1944 at the Old Vic.)

Apart from Shakespeare, Matheson Lang had many long runs in romantic melodramas such as *Pete, The Man in the Iron Mask*, *The Proud Prince*, *Mr Wu*, *The Purple Mask*, *Carnival* and *The Wandering Jew*.

Of his role in *The Devil's Disciple* he said, 'I have a keen regard for Dick Dudgeon... for in spite of his cynical embittered character, there is an underlying strain of nobility which is very fascinating to impersonate'.

34c   IVOR NOVELLO (b. Cardiff, 1893; d. 1951) as Pierre
Boucheron in *The Rat*
Publisher: J. Beagles & Co. Ltd, London
Photograph: Sasha   Postmark: 27 January 1926, London

The Welsh actor-manager, playwright and composer Ivor Novello wrote his first play, *The Rat: The Story of an Apache*, in collaboration with Constance Collier, and they both appeared in it along with Jean Webster Brough and Isobel Jeans. It was first tried out at the Theatre Royal, Brighton, on 14 January 1924, and opened at the Prince of Wales, London, on 9 June, transferring to the Garrick in September, where it ran until 31 January 1925 with a total of 282 performances. Novello appeared in the Gainsborough film of the same name in 1925; this was followed by two sequels, *The Triumph of the Rat* and *The Return of the Rat*.

34d   GEORGE ALEXANDER (b. 1858; d. 1918) as Prince Rudolf in
The Prisoner of Zenda
Publisher: J. Beagles & Co.   Photograph: Ellis & Walery

George Alexander – the English actor who was the manager of the St James' Theatre, London, from 1890 until his death – first played the dual role of Prince Rudolf/Rudolf Rassendyll at the St James' in 1896, with Evelyn Millard and Julia Neilson alternating as Princess Flavia. The swashbuckling melodrama, based by Edward Rose on Anthony Hope's novel, ran for 255 performances. So popular was it that he revived it again in 1897, 1900 and 1909, on this last occasion with Mrs Pat as Princess Flavia.

George Alexander was knighted by George V in 1911.

707 Y
BEAGLES POSTCARDS.
MR. MARTIN HARVEY
IN "THE CORSICAN BROTHERS"
ELLIS & WALERY
COPYRIGHT

a

1212 G ROTARY PHOTO, E.C.
MR. MATHESON LANG
AS "RICHARD DUDGEON" IN "THE DEVIL'S DISCIPLE."
ELLIS & WALERY, COPYRIGHT

b

PHOTO BY
SASHA

339.8.
MR. IVOR NOVELLO.
AS 'THE RAT'.
BEAGLES' POSTCARDS.

c

516 C
BEAGLES' POSTCARDS
MR. GEORGE ALEXANDER
IN "THE PRISONER OF ZENDA"
COPYRIGHT
ELLIS & WALERY

d

35a   SARAH BERNHARDT (b. 1844; d. 1923) as Marguerite
           Gautier in *La Dame aux Camélias*
           Postmark: 7 January 1902

Probably the most famous actress of all time, Sarah Bernhardt made her début at the Comédie-Française in 1862 in Racine's *Iphigénie* and was still working in the theatre in 1922. She even made a film, *La Voyante*, in the year of her death – she was too ill to go to the studios so they filmed it in her house.

Throughout her tempestuous career in Europe, North and South America, Egypt, and as far as Australia, she played hundreds of performances of *La Dame aux Camélias*, the play by Alexandre Dumas Fils, which was the favourite of her audiences everywhere. She first played the role on her American tour in 1880, then in London in 1881 and at a benefit in Paris in 1882. Then from 1884 onwards it became part of her staple repertoire. Even as an old lady with one leg amputated she played the fifth act on her tours. She played it in St Petersburg and Paris, with her husband Jacques Damala; *Punch* called her La Damala aux Camélias. She made a film of it in Paris in 1911-12, in which her technique appears exaggeratedly theatrical rather than cinematic. Her death scene was considered unbearably poignant with its fluttering hand movements and breathtaking collapse.

35b   SARAH BERNHARDT in *Théroigne de Méricourt*
           Photograph: Boyer, Paris

The French novelist and dramatist Paul Hervieu (1857-1915) was more at home with intimate plays about contemporary life and morals, and was caught out of his depth in this rambling spectacle of the French Revolution. Sarah introduced this six-act drama with its interminable speeches, huge crowd scenes and great tableaux at the Théâtre Sarah Bernhardt on 23 December 1902. She had great belief in the play and spent prodigally on its production – which she also directed. Despite her marvellous 'Mad Scene', opulent and colourful sets and the presence of that fine actor, Edouard de Max, the work was only a partial success and the settings were deemed more splendid than the play. It ran for seventy-one performances, almost but not quite paying its way at the box office, and was never seen again.

35c   RÉJANE (b. 1857; d. 1920)
           Photograph: Paul (or Saul?) Boyer, Paris   Hand-coloured

The most Parisian of actresses, born Gabrielle Réju, the vivacious Réjane was the queen of comedy. Although she played in several dramas of Sardou, including *Divorçons* and *Madame Sans-Gêne* (which she created in 1893), and had successes with *Zaza*, *Sapho*, *La Dame aux Camélias*, and even Ibsen's *A Doll's House*, it was in comedy that she shone. In her day she was favourably compared to Duse and Bernhardt, and she had successes in England and America. However, most of the comedies in which she was the toast of Paris are now forgotten, along with their authors. She barely touched the classics, but her acting was of such quality that it was said she turned paste into jewels.

In 1906 she opened the Théâtre Réjane in Paris and continued acting until the year of her death, when she appeared in Henri Bataille's *La Vierge Folle*.

35d   JANE HADING (b. 1861; d. 1933) as Madame Pompadour
           Photograph: Reutlinger, Paris   Hand-coloured

Born in Marseilles, Jane Hading first appeared on stage at the age of three. She later moved to Paris, where she was engaged first by the Théâtre du Palais-Royal, then the Théâtre de la Renaissance, the Gymnase, the Vaudeville, the Porte Saint-Martin, and later the Comédie-Française. She began as a singer of operetta and created the leading roles in Lecocq's *La Jolie Persane* (1879) and Offenbach's *Belle Lurette* (1889), both at the Renaissance. By the middle of the 'eighties she had established herself as one of the most intelligent actresses in Paris. She had great successes in *Sapho*, *Thérèse Raquin* and *Frou Frou*. She is pictured here in Emile Bergerat's five-act drama which she played with Edouard de Max at the Porte Saint-Martin in 1901. Her popularity in England was almost as great as it was in France. It was said that she understood the valuable art of listening on stage.

SARAH-BERNHARDT (LA DAME AUX CAMÉLIAS.)

a

Mme SARAH BERNHARDT
Dans "THÉROIGNE DE MÉRICOURT".

b

A Merry X'mas.

1182 Mme RÉJANE S.I.P.

c

90/12 JANE HADING S.I

d

36a   MRS LESLIE CARTER (b. 1862; d. 1937)

An unhappy Chicago society woman with blazing red hair, Mrs Leslie Carter took only her name from her divorced husband and decided to go on the stage.

Her strong emotional quality persuaded David Belasco to teach her, and she appeared under his management in 1890. In 1895 she made her presence felt as a major actress on the New York stage in Belasco's *The Heart of Maryland* which played for three years, and she made her London début at the Adelphi in December 1898 in the same play. In 1899 she made an enormous hit in Belasco's adaptation of Berton and Simon's *Zaza*, which she played at the Janick Theatre in New York, and in 1900 at the Garrick, London. In 1901 she triumphed as The Dubarry in Belasco's play of that name; it ran for three years.

Having learned all she could from Belasco, she married again and toured under her own management for more than twenty years. Her repertory consisted of Zaza, Mme Dubarry, La Tosca, Camille, Magda and Paula Tanqueray. She played Zaza in London again in 1915 and *The Lady in Red* at the London Coliseum in 1917.

36b   JULIA MARLOWE (b. 1866; d. 1950) as Barbara Frietchie
            Hand-coloured

Although born in England, Julia Marlowe went to America aged four, and must be considered an American actress. She played many roles in light opera and comedy as a child, and then made her New York début as Parthenia in *Ingomar* with instant success.

Julia Marlowe was at her best in Shakespearian roles – Juliet, Ophelia, Viola, Beatrice, Rosalind and Portia. She was well received as Lydia Languish in *The Rivals*, Lady Teazle, Julia in *The Hunchback*, Pauline in *The Lady of Lyons*, Kate Hardcastle in *She Stoops to Conquer*, Galatea in *Pygmalion and Galatea*, and in Clyde Fitch's popular American saga, *Barbara Frietchie*.

Her first marriage in 1894 to her leading man and first Romeo, Robert Taber, ended in 1900; her second husband was the actor E. H. Sothern, with whom she often appeared in *Romeo and Juliet, Hamlet, Antony and Cleopatra*, and *Macbeth*. She retired in 1915 due to ill health, but made a comeback and acted until 1924.

36c   OLGA NETHERSOLE (b. 1866; d. 1951)
            Rotary Photographic Series   Hand-coloured

Olga Nethersole first appeared in Brighton in 1887, then in London in the same year at the Grand Theatre, Islington. She played Lola Montez in *The Silver Falls* in 1888, and in 1889 had a big success in Pinero's *The Profligate*, with John Hare, at the Garrick. In 1890 she toured Australia, and after returning to London furthered her reputation by playing in Sardou's *Diplomacy* (as Dora) with the Kendals.

She made her American début in 1894, then toured constantly in England and America in *Frou Frou, La Dame aux Camélias, Carmen*, and her greatest part, *Sapho*, in Clyde Fitch's adaptation of Daudet's novel. Her torrid love scenes led to her arrest, but she was acquitted and continued with her triumphs. She added Adrienne Lecouvreur and Magda to her repertory, and was still playing Sapho when she retired in 1913.

36d   KITTY GORDON (b. 1878; d. 1974)
            Publisher: Philco Publishing Co., London
            Photograph: Bassano   Hand-coloured

Kitty Gordon first appeared in the Prince's Theatre, Bristol, in 1901, and made her name in musical comedy appearing as Olivia in *Kitty Grey* (her London début in 1901), *The Girl from Kay's* (1902), *The Duchess of Dantzic* at the Lyric Theatre (1903) as the Grand Duchess of Berg, and *Véronique* (1904) as Agatha.

She first appeared in New York at the Broadway Theatre in 1905, and continued her career in a series of long-forgotten musical comedies in both Britain and the United States.

Victor Herbert wrote for her *The Enchantress*, in which she first played in the New York Theatre in 1911 and subsequently toured. In the same year she had big successes in *The Gondoliers* and also appeared as Lady Guff Jordan (!) in *La Belle Paris*. She ventured into straight theatre, appeared a lot in vaudeville and made many successful silent films, repeating some of her stage successes. She outlived three husbands.

LESLIE CARTER

a

JULIA MARLOWE

b

OLGA NETHERSOLE

c

PHILCO SERIES No. 3005 D   KITTY GORDON

d

37a   OSCAR BEREGI (b. 1876; d. 1965) as Karl Moor in *Die Räuber*
                 Publisher: Hermann Leiser, Berlin
                 Photograph: Becker & Maass

The fine Hungarian actor Oscar Beregi joined the Teatro Comico in Budapest in 1896. During Isadora Duncan's visit to the city in 1907-08, when he was playing Romeo and Mark Antony at the National Theatre, they had a passionate affair. In *My Life* Isadora Duncan describes his 'god-like features and stature . . . tall, of magnificent proportions, a head covered with luxuriant curls, black, with purple lights in them'. He progressed to Berlin, where he became part of the Max Reinhardt troupe, and played Faust, Karl Moor in Schiller's *Die Räuber*, Goethe's Clavigo, Edmund in *King Lear*, and Death in Hofmannsthal's *Der Tor und der Tod* (1907-10). He had significant successes in the classics, both in Germany and Hungary, as Romeo, Hamlet, Othello, King Lear and Faust.

Beregi began making films in Hungary in 1916, then in Germany, Austria and Hollywood through the 'twenties and 'thirties. He lost his Hungarian citizenship because of his anti-Red sympathies and went to the United States. In the 1950s he appeared in *Anything Can Happen* (1952), *Call Me Madam* (1953) and *Desert Legion* (1953).

37b   ERNST WENDT as Karl Moor in *Die Räuber*
                 Publisher: Gebr. Schelzel, Dresden
                 Photograph: Hahn Nachfl, Dresden, 1910

Here we see the German actor Ernst Wendt in the same role in which Oscar Beregi is pictured in 37a. The play – Schiller's *Die Räuber* – has always played an important part in German theatre, although it is only rarely performed outside that country. To the rest of the world it survives (barely) as a basis for the libretto of Verdi's *I Masnadieri*, which Jenny Lind sang for the first time in London in 1847 at Her Majesty's Theatre in the Haymarket.

37c   JOSEPH KAINZ (b. Hungary, 1858; d. 1910) in *Der Meister von Palmyra* by Adolf Wilbrandt

The handsome Austrian actor Joseph Kainz was renowned for the extreme beauty and resonance of his voice. He was trained in the Meiningen company and first appeared in Vienna in 1874. While appearing in Munich in 1881 he was heard by King Ludwig II of Bavaria as Didier in Victor Hugo's *Marion Delorme*. The King, always on the lookout for the beautiful to people his fantasy world, dragged him off to the Schloss Linderhof to recite in his Blue Grotto and give other private performances for him. While on a journey to Switzerland – the King required Kainz to recite a scene from *William Tell* on top of an alp at 2 o'clock in the morning – Kainz rebelled. He did quite well with the jewels which Ludwig had showered on him, not to mention profits from the sale of the indiscreet letters he had received.

Kainz toured extensively in America and was justly famous for his Hamlet and Romeo. From 1899 until the end of his life he headed the company of the Burgtheater in Vienna.

37d   ALEXANDER MOÏSSI (b. 1880; d. 1935) as Hamlet
                 Publisher: Hermann Leiser, Berlin
                 Photograph: Becker & Maass

The Italian-German actor Moïssi made his début in Prague. In 1905 he went to Berlin, where he joined the company of Max Reinhardt at the Deutsches Theater; his finest work was here and in the next two decades his roles included Romeo, Hamlet, Oberon, the Fool in *Lear*, Faust and Mephistopheles, the Marquis of Posa in Schiller's *Don Carlos*, Danton in Büchner's (v. Hofmannsthal) *Danton's Tod*, Oedipus, Jedermann (v. Hofmannsthal), Karl in *Die Räuber*, and Oswald in *Ghosts*. In 1930 his Hamlet (in German) was seen in London.

Willi Handel wrote of him in *Max Reinhardt and His Theatre*, 'Alexander Moïssi is all lightning and flame, by blood inheritance from Dalmatia and Italy. Every sound of his voice, which is soft as a 'cello, every motion of his aristocratic slender body is dictated by the imperious impulse to live in joy and beauty'.

Oscar Beregi
als „Karl Moor."

3442
Verl. v. Herm. Leiser
Berlin, W.15.

Phot. Becker & Maass

a

HAHN NACHFL.
Dresden 1910.
503.

ERNST WENDT
als „Carl Moor" I. Akt
(Die Räuber).

b

Josef Kainz
i. Meister v. Palmyra

c

Alexander Moissi
als „Hamlet"

4915

d

38a   LYDIA MIKHAILOVNA KORENEVA as Maria Antonovna in
          Gogol's *Inspector General*
          Photograph: K. Fischer, Moscow   Hand-coloured
          Postmark: 20 October 1912, Moscow

Lydia Mikhailovna Koreneva made her début as a young girl with Stanislavsky at the Moscow Arts Theatre (of which she became an important member). She was highly esteemed for her performances in the plays of Dostoievsky and Turgenev, and appeared in Chekhov's *Uncle Vanya* with the Moscow Arts Theatre at Jolson's Fifty-ninth Street Theatre in January 1924. She was married to actor, Paul Orleneff.

38b   OLGA KNIPPER-CHEKHOVA (b. 1868; d. 1959) as Anna
          Andrevna in Gogol's *Inspector General*
          Photograph: K. Fischer, Moscow   Hand-coloured
          Postmark: 20 October 1912, Moscow

When Olga Knipper married Chekhov in 1901 she was already a leading member of the Moscow Arts Theatre. As a child she studied with the co-founder and Director of the Moscow Arts Theatre, Nemirovitch-Dantchenko, and joined the Theatre in 1898. She became the supreme interpreter of Chekhov, and created the role of Mme Ranevskaya in *The Cherry Orchard* in 1904, the year of his death.

Her first role was Irina in Tolstoi's *Tsar Feodor*. Then came her first Chekhovian role, Madame Arkadina in *The Seagull*, in 1899. She excelled as Elena in *Uncle Vanya* and Masha in *The Three Sisters* (written for her) – the latter was considered her finest part.

Olga Knipper remained with the Arts Theatre all her life and was a link with pre-Revolution theatre, carrying on the traditions of Stanislavsky. She played Mme Ranevskaya in the three-hundredth performance of her husband's *The Cherry Orchard* by the Moscow Arts Theatre in 1943, when she was seventy-five years of age.

38c   NATASHA TROUHANOVA (b. Kiev, 1885; d. Moscow, 1956)
          as the Nun in *The Miracle*
          Rotary Photographic Series   Photograph: Hoppe, London

The Miracle, presented by Charles Cochran at the Olympia in London in 1911, had some 1500 performers on stage, a chorus of 200 and an orchestra of sixty. It was a pantomimic spectacle conceived by Karl Vollmoeller and directed by Max Reinhardt. The Olympia, a huge space generally reserved for automobile shows, wrestling matches et al, was transformed by designer Ernst Stein into a great medieval church lit by a colossal gothic window of shimmering stained glass. The fine score was by Humperdinck.

Natasha Trouhanova appeared as the Nun in this pageant. She had danced at the Opéra in 1907, but was turned down by Diaghilev and developed her own style rather in the manner of Isadora Duncan. Her greatest night occurred in 1912 when she danced in the four premières of d'Indy's *Istar*, Dukas' *La Peri*, Schmitt's *La Tragédie de Salomé*, and Ravel's *Adélaide ou La Language des Fleurs*. She later married a count and retired.

38d   MAUDE ADAMS (b. 1872; d. 1953) as Peter Pan
          Publisher: Bamforth & Co., Holmfirth and New York
          Hand-coloured

The beloved American actress Maude Adams grew up on the stage playing little Eva in *Uncle Tom's Cabin* as a child, then starring opposite E. H. Sothern and John Drew.

In the theatre she is associated very much with James Barrie, as she created many of his plays in America. She played Lady Babbie in *The Little Minister* in 1897, then the title role in *Peter Pan*, which Barrie wrote with her in mind, in 1905. She played Maggie in *What Every Woman Knows*, Miss Thing in *A Kiss for Cinderella*, Phoebe in *Quality Street* and Leonora in *The Legend of Leonora*.

Maude Adams' Shakespearean roles were Juliet (opposite William Faversham), Rosalind, Viola and Portia. She also had big successes as Joan of Arc in Schiller's *Maid of Orleans*, and as the Duc de Reichstadt in Rostand's *L'Aiglon*.

Thought to be one of the kindest women in the theatre, she shunned publicity and retired at the height of her popularity.

РЕВИЗОРЪ н. в. гоголя. Моск. Худож. Театръ.
Марья Антоновна—Л. М. Коренева. 51
Изд. «Искусство и Жизнь» И. И. Корнилова и Ко. Москва.

a

РЕВИЗОРЪ н. в. гоголя. Моск. Худож. Театръ.
Анна Андреевна—О. Л. Книпперъ. 50
Изд. «Искусство и Жизнь» И. И. Корнилова и Ко, Москва.

b

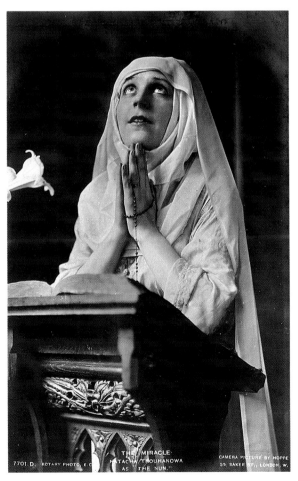

c

d

39a   MRS PATRICK CAMPBELL (b. London 1865; d. 1940) as
              Jeannie Halton in *Aunt Jeannie*
              Rotary Photographic Series   Hand-coloured
              Postmark: 10 December 1904

Mrs Pat appeared in the elegant but trifling play *Aunt Jeannie* by E. F. Benson at the Garden Theatre, New York, in September 1902, under Charles Frohman's management. It ran for only a few weeks. According to Margot Peters in *Mrs Pat* (1894) she wore the same costume in *The Foolish Virgin*, a translation of Henri Bataille's *La Vierge Folle*, in New York in 1910, which could be so. However, Mrs Pat in her autobiography identifies this very portrait as Aunt Jeannie and the postmark on the back is 1904.

39b   MRS BROWN POTTER (b. 1857; d. 1936)
              The Wrench Series   Photograph: Johnston and Hoffmann
              Hand-coloured   Postmark: 1906, Worcester

Born Cora Urquhart, Mrs Brown Potter was a rich society lady who wanted to go on the stage – and made a success of it. She had beauty, elegance and ability. After training with Belasco, she made her début in 1887 at the Haymarket, London, in the play by Wilkie Collins, *Man and Wife*.

On returning to America, she toured as Juliet with Kyrle Bellew, Pauline in *The Lady of Lyons*, Kate Hardcastle in *She Stoops to Conquer*, *The Lady of the Camellias*, and *Antony and Cleopatra*.

In 1890 Mrs Brown Potter toured Australia and the East with Bellew, and added *La Tosca* to her repertoire. After further seasons in London and the United States she returned to Australia in 1897, and in the same year appeared in London as Milady in *The Three Musketeers*. In 1904 she became Manager of London's Savoy Theatre, a venture which ended in bankruptcy. She retired in 1912.

39c   LILLIE LANGTRY (b. 1853; d. 1929)
              Rotary Photographic Series   Hand-coloured
              Postmark: 11 February 1904, Winchester

Known as the Jersey Lily, Lillie Langtry was as famous for her great beauty and scandalous behaviour as for her ability as an actress. A society belle (and the daughter of a clergyman), she became the mistress of Edward VII and caught the fancy of the public. Through her American tours and her innate business sense, she became extremely wealthy (initially helped by the jewels which the King showered on her).

Lillie Langtry first appeared on the stage in 1881 and became an expert in comedy and modern plays. Aided by an odd scandal or two, she never lost her public popularity. She had successes as Lady Macbeth, Rosalind and Cleopatra, and became a millionairess at a time when that really meant something. The public admired her as 'bad' women in plays like *The Fringe of Society* and Sidney Grundy's *The Degenerates* – which managed to get banned here and there.

An incredibly lucky woman, she had her own stable of racehorses and once broke the bank at Monte Carlo. During the First World War she worked hard for the Red Cross, and after the war she retired to the French Riviera and became an expert gardener.

39d   MAXINE ELLIOTT (b. Maine, circa 1868; d. 1940)
              Publisher: Bamforth & Co., Holmfirth and New York
              Hand-coloured

The American actress Maxine Elliott was by no means one of the greatest, but she was beautiful and well connected – one of her connections being no less than King Edward VII. However, she became quite a favourite for some twenty years, appearing in some rather terrible plays, and retired a wealthy woman.

Maxine Elliott began her career in 1890 with E. S. Willard, with whom she appeared in several forgettable plays, then joined Rose Coghlan's Company appearing in *London Assurance*, *A Woman of No Importance* and *Diplomacy*. In 1895 she joined Augustin Daly and played her first Shakespearean roles, appearing in London as Silvia (in *The Two Gentlemen of Verona*) and as Hermia, in the same year. She next teamed up with Nat Goodwin, whom she married but soon divorced, and toured with him to Australia in 1896 in some of their less choice repertoire. In 1901 she played a good Portia in London, and in the following year returned to the United States.

She opened the Maxine Elliott Theatre in 1908, but announced her retirement in 1911. She appeared intermittently until 1920 when she betook herself to Europe.

Mrs. PATRICK CAMPBELL   178 D   a

10599   Mrs. BROWN POTTER.   JOHNSTON & HOFFMAN.   b

152 C   Mrs. LANGTRY   ROTARY PHOTO. E.C   c

MISS MAXINE ELLIOTT   d

40a   MAUD JEFFRIES (b. 1869; d. 1946) in *The Sign of the Cross*
                 Publisher: J. Beagles & Co.
                 Photograph: W. & D. Downey   Hand-coloured

Born on a cotton plantation in Mississippi, Maud Jeffries joined Augustin Daly's Company in New York in 1889. She was engaged by Wilson Barrett and played his repertoire in the mammoth melodramas of the period. She was the first Mercia in *The Sign of the Cross* (Wilson Barrett) which she played throughout the world. She toured Australia with Barrett in 1897.

Back in London Maud Jeffries appeared with Beerbohm Tree in *Herod* (Stephen Philips) at Her Majesty's in 1900, and toured extensively as Roma in *The Eternal City* (Hall Caine) in 1903-04. In Australia again she was Julius Knight's leading lady in various plays. She married a wealthy Australian settler and retired from the stage in 1906.

40b   MRS MAESMORE MORRIS
                 Publisher: C.B. & Co. Ltd., Australia; Graphic Series
                 Photograph: Talma & Co., Melbourne and Sydney
                 Hand-coloured

The grandly named Mrs Maesmore Morris was born Gertrude Wilmot in England. She went to Melbourne with her father, a doctor, and there married Mr Morris in 1894. Her stage career began with Charles Hawtrey in Australia, playing several roles in *The Sign of the Cross*.

Arriving in London in 1899, she was subsequently engaged at the St James', first as Julie Opp's understudy in *The Prisoner of Zenda*. She then appeared in *Rupert of Henzau* with George Alexander, and starred with H. B. Irving in *The Plot of His Story* by Mrs Oscar Beringer. After playing at various theatres throughout England, she returned to dazzle the colonies. She appeared throughout Australia in her usual repertoire, then retired as a naval lieutenant's wife circa 1907.

40c   MISS TITTELL BRUNE (b. San Francisco, 1883; d. 1978 [?])
                 Photograph: Talma & Co., Melbourne and Sydney
                 Hand-coloured

Minnie Tittell Brune first appeared on the stage aged four at the California Theatre in San Francisco – as Tim in *Lights o' London*. After much repertory experience in stock companies she played in New York (1893-95) and then toured with Charles Frohman. Her stardom began in Australia and New Zealand. Her success in both countries was second only to Sarah Bernhardt's. (Bernhardt was in fact her idol.)

Following her début in *L'Aiglon* (Rostand) – an immediate triumph – she also played *La Dame aux Camélias*, *The Second Mrs Tanqueray*, Juliet, *Peter Pan*, and various other roles.

In 1909 she went to London and was an instant success, although not the star she had been down-under. She played in *Dr Jekyll and Mr Hyde* at the Queen's Theatre in 1910, and Roma in Hall Caine's *Eternal Question* at the Coronet in 1911. In 1913 she played *Nel Gwynne* and Rebecca in *Ivanhoe*, and in 1917 she toured as Annie Moran in *Bracelets*. She appears to have made her farewell to the theatre as Mme Cavallini in *Romance* in 1921.

40d   NELLIE STEWART (b. Sydney 1858; d. Sydney, 1931)
                 Photograph: Talma & Co., Melbourne and Sydney
                 Postmark: 24 September 1904

Australia's idol Nellie Stewart, an actress and singer of great versatility, appeared on the stage from childhood. She made many great 'hits' in operetta, introducing several pieces of Gilbert and Sullivan into Australia, and her career also included the role of Marguerite in *Faust*. In the 'seventies and 'eighties she sang the popular comic operas of the day.

Nellie Stewart's first London appearance was in a burlesque *Blue Eyed Susan* at the Prince of Wales (1892), but her big successes were the Drury Lane pantomimes of 1898 and 1899 where she played principal boy in *The Forty Thieves* and *Jack in the Beanstalk*. For the most part her career was in Australia and New Zealand, where she was dearly loved and where she played *Zaza*, *La Dame aux Camélias*, *The Dubarry*, *Trilby*, *Pretty Peggy*, *When Knighthood Was in Flower*, and endless revivals of *Sweet Nell of Old Drury* – the public's favourite.

No. 530
J B & Co
MISS MAUD JEFFRIES.
AS "MERCIA" IN "THE SIGN OF THE CROSS."
W. & D. DOWNEY.

a

R. 51   MRS. MAESMORE MORRIS.   C.B. & CO. LD.

b

Miss Tittell Brune

c

Miss Nellie Stewart

d

41a   DOROTHEA BAIRD (b. 1875; d. 1933) as Trilby
Publisher: J. Beagles & Co., London   Postmark: 16 May 1904

The daughter-in-law of Henry Irving, Dorothea Baird participated in many important theatrical events in her twenty-year career. As a young member of Ben Greet's company she began in Shakespeare, but created a sensation when she appeared at the Haymarket with Beerbohm Tree in the title role of George Du Maurier's *Trilby* (30 October 1895). In London it ran for 254 performances in the first season. In 1898 she was at the Lyceum with Henry Irving in *The Medicine Man*, *The Merchant of Venice*, *The Lyons Mail*, *The Bells* and *Louis XI*.

In 1908 she toured with her husband, H. B. Irving, playing Francesca to his Paolo, and Henrietta Maria in *Charles I*. For the remainder of her career the splendid pair toured together in England, America and Australia (1911).

41b   GLADYS COOPER (b. 1889; d. 1971)
Rotary Photograph, London

Gladys Cooper began as the beauteous queen of postcards and ended up a grand old lady of the British theatre – a Dame of the British Empire, playing in a revival of *The Chalk Garden* in her eighty-fourth year.

As a young actress Gladys Cooper worked with Seymour Hicks and then joined George Edwardes' company at the Gaiety Theatre, playing in *The Girls of Gottenberg* (1907), *Havana* (1908) and *Our Miss Gibbs* (1909). In 1909 she played Sadie van Tromp in *The Dollar Princess* at Daly's, but moved into straight theatre with a revival of *The Importance of Being Earnest* at the St James' with George Alexander.

A large space would be needed to list all her roles. She managed her own theatre and played in four premières by Somerset Maugham. She was not afraid of the repertory and played *Peter Pan*, *Magda* and *The Second Mrs Tanqueray*. She divided the second half of her life between London and America, where she made some thirty films including *Rebecca*, *Now Voyager*, *Separate Tables* and *My Fair Lady*.

41c   JULIA NEILSON (b. 1868; d. 1957)
Publisher: Raphael Tuck & Sons   Photocrome 'Celebrities
of the Stage'   Photograph: Lafayette

Julia Neilson made her début playing Cynisca to Mary Anderson's Galatea in W. S. Gilbert's *Pygmalion and Galatea* at the Lyceum in March 1888, and later played Galatea to Lewis Waller's Pygmalion at the Savoy. She joined Beerbohm Tree's company, staying with him for five years, and married Fred Terry, younger brother of Ellen. In 1895 she played Lady Chiltern in *An Ideal Husband* at the Criterion with Waller. She toured America with John Hare in 1895-96, playing Agnes in *The Notorious Mrs Ebbsmith* (Pinero). Returning to England she played Princess Flavia to George Alexander's *Prisoner of Zenda*, Rosalind in *As You Like It*, and Beatrice in *Much Ado About Nothing*.

The famous partnership with her husband began in 1900 with *Sweet Nell of Old Drury*, and they had many successes together in romantic dramas such as *The Scarlet Pimpernel*, *Dorothy o' the Hall*, *The Popinjay*, *Henry of Navarre* and *Matt of Merrymount*; they toured in many countries until her husband's death in 1933.

41d   LILY ELSIE (b. 1886; d. 1962)
Rotary Opalette Series

Lily Elsie made her first stage appearance as a child in 1892 in *Red Riding Hood* and then toured the music halls as Little Elsie. After several years of pantos she made her first big success as Soo-Soo in the musical comedy, *A Chinese Honeymoon*.

Her reputation was assured forever when she created the English version of Lehár's *The Merry Widow* at Daly's on 25 September 1907, with Joe Coyne and Robert Michaelis as Danilo, W. H. Berry as Nisch and George Groves as Baron Popoff. It ran for over two years and 779 performances. She followed this triumph with Leo Fall's *The Dollar Princess* (448 performances) in 1909, and in 1911-12 Oscar Strauss' *A Waltz Dream* (106 performances) and *The Count of Luxembourg* (339 performances). These were her major successes, but she was heard in London as late as 1927 in Robert Stoltz' *The Blue Train*.

MISS DOROTHEA BAIRD.

a

With all Kind Thoughts.

b

MISS JULIA NEILSON

c

LILY ELSIE.

d

42a   EMIL JANNINGS (b. 1884; d. 1950) as Henry VIII
             Ross Series   Photograph: Rembrandt

Emil Jannings was one of the big silent stars of the German cinema. He was on stage from childhood and joined Max Reinhardt in 1906. Initially lured to the screen by Ernst Lubitsch in 1914, he made more than fifty films, many directed by von Sternberg, Murnau and Lubitsch. He made seven epics with Lubitsch between 1917 and 1920; these included *Madame Dubarry* (1919) and *Anne Boleyn* (1920). In America between 1927 and 1929, he made six films for Paramount.

On returning to Germany he played Professor Unrath, Marlene Dietrich's victim in *The Blue Angel*, the role for which he is most remembered today. During the war he made several German propaganda films and he retired to Austria in 1945, *persona non grata* in the industry because of his Hitlerian sympathies.

42b   HERBERT BEERBOHM TREE (b. 1853; d. 1917) as Svengali
             Publisher: Rotary   Photograph: R. C. Turner, London & Hull

The English actor-manager Herbert Beerbohm Tree specialised in the grandiose and the fantastic. His greatest success was as Svengali in *Trilby* which he created in 1896, during his term of ten years as manager of the Haymarket. With the profits he built Her Majesty's Theatre and continued the Irving tradition of spectacular drama from 1897 until 1912. In 1909 he was knighted by King Edward VII.

Some of Tree's memorable roles were Falstaff, King John, Petruchio, Mark Antony, Malvolio, Shylock, Macbeth, Herod, Ulysses, Prince Dmitri Nehludoff in *Resurrection*, Fagin, Nero, Colonel Newcombe and Sir Peter Teazle. He was a master of make-up, with the ability to completely alter his appearance, and excelled in the macabre.

42c   MICHAEL REDGRAVE (b. 1908; d. 1985)
             Photograph: Howard Coster   Autographed

After beginning his working life as a schoolteacher, Michael Redgrave made his professional début at the Liverpool Playhouse in 1934. He made his London début at the Old Vic in *Love's Labours Lost* in 1936, and had great success as Orlando in *As You Like It* with Edith Evans as Rosalind.

Redgrave had continued success in English theatre in the next decade and a half – his Hamlet was much praised, and he played it in Switzerland, Holland, Denmark, and later in Russia. In 1951 he went to the Shakespearean theatre in Stratford-on-Avon, where Prospero was considered one of his best roles. In his later life he acted constantly, touring America and Australia, and directed many plays and two operas at Glyndebourne.

Between 1936 and 1971 Redgrave appeared in many films, notably *The Lady Vanishes* (1938), *The Stars Look Down* (1939), *The Way to the Stars* and *Dead of Night* (1945), *The Captive Heart* and *The Years Between* (1946), *Fame is the Spur* and *Mourning Becomes Elektra* (1947), *The Browning Version* (1950), *The Importance of Being Earnest* (1952), *The Dam Busters* (1955), and *The Quiet American* (1958). In 1959 he received a knighthood.

42d   LAURENCE OLIVIER (b. 1907) as Hamlet
             Autographed

Very much a part of the tradition of the great British actors, Olivier is one of the most versatile, fascinating and lasting of all. He will be remembered for his definitive performances as Hamlet, Romeo, Henry V, Richard III, Antony, King Lear and Titus Andronicus. He has been at the head of the Old Vic, the Chichester Festival Theatre and the National Theatre.

Olivier's non-Shakespearean repertoire has included many triumphs. He created Noël Coward's *Private Lives* in 1930, was splendid as Sheridan's Mr Puff and Sir Peter Teazle, Oedipus Rex, and in Rattigan's *The Sleeping Prince*, Osborne's *The Entertainer*, Anouilh's *Becket* and Astrov in *Uncle Vanya* – all important in theatre history.

Amongst his innumerable movies, which include a high percentage of very good ones, perhaps the most memorable are *Wuthering Heights* (1939), *Pride and Prejudice* (1940), *Rebecca* (1940), *Lady Hamilton* (1941), *Henry V* (1944), *Hamlet* (1948), *Richard III* (1956), *The Prince and the Showgirl* (1958), *The Entertainer* (1960), *Sleuth* (1972) and *Boys from Brazil* (1978). He continues well into the 1980s with the television series *Brideshead Revisited* (1981) and other fascinating cameo appearances on television and in film.

Olivier has been married to three actresses – Jill Esmond, Vivien Leigh and Joan Plowright. He was knighted in 1947 and given a life peerage in 1971.

Emil Jannings
als König Heinrich VIII im Film
„Anna Boleyn"

Verlag „ROSS", Berlin SW68

a

106 E   MR. BEERBOHM TREE   ROTARY PHOTO. E.C.
As "SVENGALI."

b

MICHAEL REDGRAVE   PHOTOGRAPH BY HOWARD COSTER, F.R.S.A.

c

LAURENCE OLIVIER
as Hamlet.

d

43a   MARIE TEMPEST (b. 1864; d. 1942)
                 Empire Series, London   Hand-coloured

The English actress Marie Tempest was initially a singer of some note, then made a transition to straight acting roles with the turn of the century. She appeared as Nell Gwynn, Peg Woffington and Becky Sharp, directed in each of these roles by Dion Boucicault. She had a hit with *The Marriage of Kitty*, adapted from the French for her by her second husband, Cosmo Gordon-Lennox, in 1902; she played in this on and off for thirty years. Somerset Maugham's *Mrs Dot* (1908) and his *Penelope* (1909) were two of her favourite parts.

During the First World War she made a mammoth world tour with her third husband, the actor W. Grahame Browne, through America, Africa, the Far East, Australia and New Zealand. Back in London, she created Noël Coward's *Hay Fever* in 1925 – this ran for 337 performances.

Throughout her long career Marie Tempest achieved great popularity in drawing-room comedy, in which she could demonstrate her chic comedic flair and immaculate timing. She was created a Dame of the British Empire in 1937, aged seventy-one, and her last and successful performances were in Dodie Smith's *Dear Octopus* at the Queen's Theatre in 1938.

43b   LILY BRAYTON (b. 1876; d. 1953)
                 Publisher: J. Beagles & Co., London
                 Photograph: Lallie Charles   Autographed

Lily Brayton made her first appearances with the Benson Company in 1896, playing numerous Shakespearean parts. In 1900 she played Marianne in *Herod*, opposite Beerbohm Tree and a splendid Viola in *Twelfth Night*. Her interesting roles in the early years of the century included Katusha in *Resurrection*, Yo-San in *The Darling of the Gods*, and Katharina in *The Taming of the Shrew*.

From 1907 Lily Brayton appeared under the management of her husband, Oscar Asche, performing with him as Rosalind in *As You Like It*, Desdemona in *Othello*, Katharina, Portia, and Mistress Ford in *The Merry Wives*. They toured Australia in 1909, and back in London she appeared as Clotilde in *Count Hannibal* as well as playing her preferred Shakespearean parts. In 1911 she appeared with her husband in the oriental spectacular *Kismet*, also directed by him; this, with its revivals, was to make their first fortune. In 1912-13 they made another tour of Australia, and also toured South Africa.

In 1916 they produced *Chin-Chin-Chow*, at His Majesty's Theatre, which broke all records and played from August 1916 without pause until July 1921. There were 2238 performances and Lily Brayton played the part of Zahrat-al-Kulub almost 2000 times. Her last performance on the stage was as Portia in 1932.

43c   MARY ANDERSON (b. 1859; d. 1940)
                 Publisher: J. Beagles & Co., London
                 Photograph: Langmer   Hand-coloured
                 Autographed (Mary Anderson de Navarro)

Mary Anderson, a woman of great beauty and allure, made her début as Juliet in 1875 at the Louisville Theatre at the age of sixteen. In 1877 she played Pauline in Lytton's *The Lady of Lyons* in New York, Parthenia in *Ingomar*, and Julie in Sheridan Knowles' *The Hunchback* – all parts which remained in her repertory. She made her London début as Parthenia at the Lyceum in 1833, played Rosalind at Stratford-on-Avon in 1887, and was the first actress to double the parts of Perdita and Hermione in *A Winter's Tale*. She retired just before her marriage in 1890.

43d   EVELYN MILLARD (b. 1873; d. 1941)
                 Publisher: Aristophot Co. Ltd, London
                 Photograph: Rita Martin   Hand-coloured

The handsome English actress Evelyn Millard is best remembered as leading lady to the matinee idols George Alexander and Lewis Waller. After a few years learning her craft in the provinces, she joined George Alexander – first on tour and then at the St James' Theatre where, between 1894 and 1896, she appeared as Dulcie Larondie in Henry Arthur Jones' *The Masqueraders*, Mary Brazier in Henry James' *Guy Domville*, Cecily Cardew in the première of *The Importance of Being Earnest*, Paula in *The Second Mrs Tanqueray*, Lady Harding in Haddon Chambers' *The Idler*, and Princess Flavia in *The Prisoner of Zenda*.

After working for some time with Beerbohm Tree and then with Charles Frohman, she returned to the St James' for *Paolo and Francesca* with George Alexander. In 1904 she began an important partnership with Lewis Waller, initially at the Imperial and later at the Lyric. In 1908 she began to appear under her own management, first at the Garrick, then at the Criterion, and later at the New Theatre.

MARIE TEMPEST

a

MISS LILY BRAYTON

b

MISS MARY ANDERSON.

c

Evelyn Millard

d

Shakespeare   **44a**   MRS PATRICK CAMPBELL (b. London, 1865; d. 1940) as Juliet
                            Photograph: Alfred Ellis & Walery, London   Autographed

The beautiful, tempestuous, English-Italian 'Mrs Pat' often lacked a sense of her own responsibility. When she wanted to, her acting was superb – she was frequently compared to Duse and Bernhardt – but sometimes she just couldn't be bothered. She was wonderful in Pinero's *The Second Mrs Tanqueray*, which she created at the St James' in 1893, and also in Pinero's *The Notorious Mrs Ebbsmith* at the Garrick in 1895. In the same year she played Juliet to Forbes-Robertson's Romeo at the Lyceum – this was not a critical success but the public liked it. Her other great parts were Sudermann's Magda, Melisande (which she played to the Pelleas of both Martin Harvey and Sarah Bernhardt) and Ibsen's Hedda Gabler.

George Bernard Shaw wrote the part of Eliza Doolittle for her in *Pygmalion*; this she created in 1914 with enormous success (she was forty-nine at the time). In 1929 she played her last London run: 227 wonderful performances in *The Matriarch*.

Mrs Pat later went to Hollywood, where she made a few poor films in character roles and made more than a few enemies with her sharp but often amusing tongue. She is remembered as a fine interpreter of Ibsen, Shaw, Pinero and Maeterlinck. (See also **39a**.)

44b   MRS KENDAL (b. 1848; d. 1935) as Mistress Ford
              Rotary Photographic Series   Postmark: 1907, Dover

Madge Robertson already had a reputation as a major actress before she married W. H. Kendal. As Mr and Mrs Kendal they became one of the great acting partnerships – though she tended to overshadow her husband, especially in comedy where she excelled. The couple made several enormously successful tours.

Mrs Kendal created many pieces by W. S. Gilbert, but two of her big successes were in plays of Sardou: Dora in *Diplomacy* and Lady Orman in *Peril*, an adaptation of *Nos Intimes*. She played Mistress Ford to Ellen Terry's Mistress Page at His Majesty's Theatre in 1902, with Beerbohm Tree as the fat knight.

Mrs Kendal ruled her company with a rod of iron. She was much respected in the profession and was created 'Dame' in 1927.

44c   VIOLET VANBRUGH (b. 1867; d. 1947) as Queen Katherine in
              Henry VIII
              Publisher: J. Beagles & Co., London
              Photograph: Daily Mirror Studio

Although the aristocratic-looking Violet Vanbrugh began her career in burlesque at Toole's theatre in 1886, she was to become a distinguished tragedian. Early on she toured America with the Kendals, subsequently returning to England to join Henry Irving at the Lyceum. Her first role in *Henry VIII* was that of Anne Boleyn, but she also understudied Ellen Terry as Queen Katherine. She later played Queen Katherine at His Majesty's with Herbert Beerbohm Tree (1910), as well as Lady Macbeth – two of her finest roles. She married the actor Arthur Bourchier, and together they made a very successful acting partnership.

44d   CONSTANCE COLLIER (b. 1878; d. 1955) as Cleopatra
              Rotary Photographic Series   Photograph: Bassano
              Hand-coloured

The English actress Constance Collier began her career as Peasblossom in *A Midsummer Night's Dream* aged three, and throughout her long career she played many Shakespearean roles. After an apprenticeship as one of George Edwardes' young ladies she spent six years (from 1901) with Herbert Beerbohm Tree's company, where she performed four of her great non-Shakespearean roles: Roma in Hall Caine's *Eternal City*, Nancy in *Oliver Twist*, Poppea in Stephen Philips' *Nero*, and George du Maurier's Trilby. In 1906 she played Cleopatra to Tree's Antony; they also performed these roles in Berlin before the German Emperor. Constance Collier's other roles included Thaïs, adapted from Anatole France, and the Duchess in George du Maurier's *Peter Ibbetson*.

After touring constantly in her favourite parts, she finally settled in Hollywood (where she had been making films since 1916). She appeared in over thirty films, the last in 1950, playing diverse parts – many of them autocratic, sharp-tongued and eccentric dowagers. One I would love to see is the 1922 *Bohemian Girl* in which she played the Gypsy Queen with Gladys Cooper as Arline, Ivor Novello as Thaddeus, and Ellen Terry as the Nurse!

Mrs. PATRICK CAMPBELL.

a

197 D   MRS. KENDAL   ROTARY PHOTO, E.C.
As " MISTRESS FORD"

b

90.B.   MISS VIOLET VANBRUGH.   BEAGLES' POSTCARDS.
AS 'QUEEN KATHARINE' IN 'KING HENRY VIII.'

c

4039 K   MISS CONSTANCE COLLIER,   ROTARY PHOTO. E.C.
AS "CLEOPATRA."

d

45a   LEWIS WALLER (b. 1850; d. 1915) as Henry V
              Rotary Photo   Photograph: Langfier, London
              Autographed

Lewis Waller's great production of *Henry V* opened at the Lyric Theatre on 25 November 1908 and ran for seventy-two performances until 30 January 1909. He had many successes in Shakespearean roles, especially Romeo, Othello, Brutus, Lysander and Faulconbridge.

He began his career in J. L. Toole's company in 1883 and was later engaged by the great Polish actress, Helena Modjeska, with whom he played Orlando in *As You Like It* and smaller parts in *Mary Stuart*, *Heartsease*, *La Dame Aux Camélias* and *Adrienne Lecouvreur*.

Waller worked for some time with Wilson Barrett's company, then with John Hare, Lillie Langtry and Beerbohm Tree. He had successes as Captain Absolute in *The Rivals*, Lord Illingworth in *A Woman of No Importance*, and Sir Robert Chiltern in *An Ideal Husband*. But he is probably most remembered for his roles in the romantic costume dramas such as *Monsieur Beaucaire*, *Mlle Mars* (Napolean), *Robin Hood*, *The Three Musketeers*, *A Marriage of Convenience*, *Harlequin King*, *Brigadier Gerard*, *The Duke's Motto*, *A White Man*, *The Explorer*, *Clancarty* and *The Fires of Fate*. (See also **20a**.)

45b   FORBES-ROBERTSON (b. 1853; d. 1937) as Romeo
              Rotary Photo, London   Autographed

I could not even attempt to cover the vast career of the great actor-manager Johnston Forbes-Robertson, the most romantic actor of his day and perhaps the greatest Hamlet ever.

In the early part of his career he played Romeo, first in 1880 with Helena Modjeska, then with Mary Anderson, and finally with Mrs Patrick Campbell (1896).

William Winter says of him in *Vagrant Memories*, 'His elocution was deliciously melodious, his style gracefully pliant', and of his Romeo with Modjeska: 'Because of his true ideal winning personality, natural ardour and exquisite refinement, he was a peculiarly fit representative'. Forbes-Robertson received a knighthood in 1913, during the last week of his farewell season at Drury Lane.

45c   OSCAR ASCHE (b. 1871; d. 1936) as Othello
              Rotary Photo   Photograph: Rita Marlin

Oscar Asche is best remembered today for the astonishing five-year run of his oriental concoction, *Chu-Chin-Chow* (1916-21) – 'more navel than millinery', said Beerbohm Tree – and his other Eastern epic *Kismet*. He was born in Geelong, Victoria, and went to England at the end of his school days. After spending eight years with F. R. Benson playing Shakespeare, he then acted with Tree. His best parts were Petrucchio, Falstaff, Bottom, Shylock and Claudius. He toured the world with his wife, Lily Brayton, returning to Australia for several seasons. A fine actor, Oscar Asche worked right up until his death. He made silent films of *Don Quixote* and *Scrooge*.

45d   MATHESON LANG (b. 1879; d. 1948) as Hamlet
              Rotary Photo   Photograph: Foulsham & Banfield (1910)

In the balmy days when there were several splendid Hamlets, Matheson Lang was certainly the most handsome of all and compared well with the best actors. Following his successful Romeo in 1908, he played Hamlet at the Lyceum Theatre from 13 March 1909 for sixty-three performances (although there wasn't another star name in the cast). He was invited to play the part at Stratford-on-Avon and it remained his favourite role. In his earlier days he had acquired ample experience of the play, appearing in it as the First and Second Actor, the Priest, Bernardo, Marcellus, Guildenstern, Laertes, Polonius, Claudius, Voltimand, and Fortinbras' Captain. He essayed his first Hamlet on a tour of the West Indies and South America in 1905 with F. R. Benson's company.

107 Q MR. LEWIS WALLER as "Henry V." ROTARY PHOTO. E.C.

a

FORBES ROBERTSON

b

1236 D MR. OSCAR ASCHE. ROTARY PHOTO. E.C.
AS "OTHELLO."

c

2391 F ROTARY PHOTO. E.C. MR. MATHESON LANG FOULSHAM & BANFIELD
AS "HAMLET."

d

46a, 46b, 46c, 46d

These four chromolithographed cards of Shakespearean characters are very typical of the beautiful illustrative work done around the turn of the century.

The two scenes from *Romeo and Juliet* were made in Germany. The portrait of Orlando in *As You Like It* is one of a series – *Shakespeare's Heroes and Heroines* – published by Raphael Tuck & Sons; it is signed, H. Saunders. The portrait of Jessica and Lorenzo (*Merchant of Venice*) has no accompanying information.

Romeo und Julie.

a

Romeo und Julie.

b

Orlando.

"O Rosalind! these trees shall be my books,
And in their barks my thoughts I'll character".

As you like it, Act III, Sc. II.

c

Jessica & Lorenzo

d

Musical
Comedy

47a   ANNA HELD (b. Paris, 1873; d. 1918)
Publisher: H. V. & Co.   Hand-coloured
Postmark: 1908, Hampstead

The tiny Anna Held, with her eighteen-inch waist, was already a star earning huge sums at the Palace
Theatre, London, when Florenz Ziegfeld discovered her and took her to America. He starred her in *Papa's
Wife*, *The Little Duchess*, *Mlle Napoleon*, *The Parisian Model* and *Miss Innocence*. Singing with Gallic charm
'Won't you come and play wiz me?' and 'I just can't make my eyes behave', she enchanted the public who
were already intrigued by rumours of her milk baths and general naughtiness.

Orphaned at twelve, Anna Held worked her way up from the chorus to stardom, and married Ziegfeld
(whom she later divorced). She was portrayed in the film *The Great Ziegfeld* (1936) by Luise Rainer.

47b   EVELYN NESBIT (b. 1884; d. 1967)
Publisher: Rafael Tuck & Son   Hand-coloured
Postmark: 1908

The fame of Evelyn Nesbit rests firmly upon the murder trials in which she was involved when her rich but
none-too-stable Philadelphian husband, Harry Thaw, shot one of her lovers – the brilliant architect
Standford White. It came out in court that Mr White used to pose her naked in a red velvet swing for his
titillation, and *The Girl in the Red Velvet Swing* was the title of the film about her life in which Joan Collins
starred in 1955. Initially a model and chorus girl, Evelyn Nesbit made three movies – *Threads of Destiny*
(1914), *Redemption* (1917) and *Hidden Woman* (1922) – and sustained a very lucrative vaudeville career into
the 'twenties.

47c   BILLIE BURKE (b. 1885; d. 1970) in *The Belle of Mayfair*
Publisher: Davidson Brothers, London
Photograph: Bassano   Hand-coloured

The twittering, dithering, enchanting Billie Burke began her career in vaudeville and later played in
musical comedy. She took over Leslie Stuart's musical comedy *The Belle of Mayfair* from Phyllis Dare in
1907, and was immediately engaged by Charles Hawtrey. After making her New York début at the Empire
with John Drew in *My Wife* (1907), she had a huge success in Somerset Maugham's *Mrs Dot* at the New
York Lyceum in 1909.

Billie Burke had many stage successes in London, New York and on tour, but gradually moved into
films, of which her first was *Gloria's Romance* in 1916. After a dozen or so silents, she made innumerable
talking pictures in which she generally played her endearing self. Some to be remembered are *A Bill of
Divorcement* (1932), *Dinner at Eight* (1933), *A Feather in Her Hat* (1935), *Topper* (1937), *Young in Heart*
(1938), *The Wizard of Oz* (1939), *The Man Who Came to Dinner* (1941), *The Cheaters* (1945) and *Father of
the Bride* (1950); her last film was *Pepe* in 1960.

47d   LILLIAN RUSSELL (b. 1861; d. 1922) as Lady Teazle
Publisher: Bamforth & Co.   Photograph: Falk
Postmark: 1908, Indiana

Lillian Russell, 'The American Beauty', studied to be an opera singer but made her début in vaudeville at
Tony Pastor's theatre on Broadway in 1880. Then came an excursion into comic opera. In 1884 she
thought she had married her second husband, the composer Edward Solomon who wrote two light operas
for her, *Virginia* and *Polly*, which she played in London. Her 'husband', however, had married her
bigamously and was claimed by a music-hall singer, Lillie Grey.

Lillian Russell returned to New York, where she appeared in Offenbach's *The Brigands*, *The Grand
Duchess*, *La Belle Hélène* and *La Périchole*, as well as Lococq's *Pepita* and *Giroflé-Girofla*. She joined Weber
and Field's company in 1900 and had a huge success in *Lady Teazle* (1904), a comic opera based on *The
School for Scandal*. The beautiful, ample-bosomed, tiny-waisted prima donna was a phenomenon in her
time and much beloved of the public. She spent the rest of her life in vaudeville (in which she was paid a
fortune), went through two more husbands, and had a much publicised liaison with the millionaire,
'Diamond Jim' Brady. She made one film – her 1907 stage success, *Wildfire* – in 1915 with Lionel
Barrymore.

a

MISS FLORENCE EVELYN NESBITT
(MRS. HARRY THAW)

H. V. & CO.

b

Series 2401 Miss Billie Burke. Davidson Brothers
ONDON

c

MISS LILIAN RUSSELL

Photo only
Copyright by Falk

d

48a   PHYLLIS DARE (b. 1890; d. 1975)
         Rotary Photographic Series   Hand-coloured
         Postmark: 12 March 1918, Melbourne

At nine years of age, Phyllis Dare was one of the Babes in the Wood with her sister Zena, and at ten she played Ib with Martin Harvey in *Ib and Little Christina* at the Prince of Wales in London. She continued in plays and pantos, appearing with Seymour Hicks in *Bluebell in Fairyland* (1901) at the Vaudeville, and taking over from Ellaline Terriss in *The Catch of the Season* (1905). She had big successes in *The Belle of Mayfair, Cinderella, The Dairymaids*, and in Lionel Monkton's *Arcadians* (1901) at the Shaftesbury which ran for 810 performances. Her other hits were in *The Sunshine Girl, The Dancing Mistress, The Girl from Utah* and *The Quaker Girl*, all favourite musical comedies of the time.

   She appeared in musicals with odd forays into straight theatre throughout the 'twenties, 'thirties and 'forties. Her last appearances were in Ivor Novello's *King's Rhapsody*, in which both she and her sister starred; this opened in London in 1949 and ran for over two years.

48b   MARIE STUDHOLME (b. 1875; d. 1930)
         Publisher: J. Beagles & Co., London
         Photograph: Kilpatrick   Hand-coloured.

The glamorous, ever-smiling Marie Studholme was one of the most photographed beauties of her day. Her first appearance in musical comedy was in 1891. George Edwardes engaged her in 1893 for *A Gaiety Girl*, and she went on to star in several long-running successes: *The Artist's Model* (1895), *The Geisha* (1896), *The Greek Slave* (1898), *San Toy* (1899), *The Messenger Boy* (1900), *The Toreador* (1901), *The Orchid* (1903), *Lady Madcap* (1906), *Miss Hook of Holland* (1907) and *My Mimosa Maid* (1908). She toured in some of her favourites as far as South Africa.

48c   MAUDE FEALY (b. 1883; d. 1971)
         Publisher: The Rapid Photo Printing Co. Ltd, London
         Postmark: 1905

The beautiful actress Maude Fealy was born in Memphis, Tennessee, and was on stage from the age of three. Her New York début was in *Quo Vadis* at the New York Theatre in 1900; William Gillette saw her and engaged her to play Alice Faulkner in *Sherlock Holmes*, which she played at the London Lyceum for 213 performances (1901-02). Back in America she was leading lady to E. S. Willard, appearing notably in *The Cardinal*. Henry Irving engaged her in 1904-05, when she played Rosamund in *Becket*, Julie Lesurque in *The Lyons' Mail*, and Marie in *Louis XI*.

   For the remainder of her career Maude Fealy stayed in the United States, appearing sometimes with Nat Goodwin's company, and kept working until the First World War. She made a few unsuccessful films. Her extraordinary London successes, when innumerable postcards of her were published, were perhaps largely due to her youthful beauty and apparent vulnerability.

48d   ZENA DARE (b. 1887; d. 1975)
         Publisher: Rapid Photo Printing Co., London   Postmark: 1909

Zena Dare's career started at the same time as that of her sister Phyllis (they appeared as Babes in the Wood). She was to continue in the theatre until, as a remarkable old lady, she played Mrs Higgins in *My Fair Lady*; she appeared in this role for five years at Drury Lane, and then toured for another year until her retirement in 1965.

   In her youth Zena Dare had many successes in pantomime, as well as in her hits *Lady Madcap, The Gay Gordons*, and *The Dashing Little Duke*. After having retired from the stage on her marriage in 1911, she returned in 1926 in the straight play *The Last of Mrs Cheyney*. She had major successes in the plays of Ivor Novello, notably *Careless Rapture* which she played at Drury Lane in 1936, and *Full House* in which she and her sister appeared together in 1940. She played Mrs Darling in *Peter Pan* for several Christmases, and was back with Ivor Novello in 1945 in *Perchance to Dream* and *King's Rhapsody* (1949-51).

1846 Y   MISS PHYLLIS DARE.   ROTARY PHOTO. E.C.

a

842.   MISS MARIE STUDHOLME.   J.B.&C9.

b

Miss Maud Fealy.

c

Miss Zena Dare.

d

49a   PAULINE CHASE (b. 1885; d. 1962)
               Publisher: Philco Series   Photograph: Johnston & Hoffmann
               Hand-coloured

The American actress Pauline Chase is remembered for her many performances in London as Peter Pan.

James Barrie's fairy play was first produced at the Duke of York's theatre on 27 December 1904, and ran for 150 performances. Nina Boucicault created the title role and the first twin was played by Pauline Chase. The following Christmas, Cissie Loftus played Peter Pan and Pauline repeated her initial role. At the third revival, Christmas 1906, Pauline Chase played her first Peter Pan – which was so stunning that she repeated it every Christmas for the next eight years until the beginning of 1914, performing the part well over 600 times. She also played it in Paris at the Vaudeville in June of 1907 and 1908. In her last revival, in 1913, the part of Slightly was played by Master Noël Coward.

49b   ADA REEVE (b. 1876; d. 1966)
               Publisher: Philco Series
               Photograph: Johnston and Hoffmann   Hand-coloured
               Postmark: 12 July 1905, Weston-Super-Mere

Although not one of the great beauties of her day, Ada Reeve made up for it with charm and verve. She made her début as Willie Carlyle in East Lynne in 1882, and in her early days had many successes in boy parts. Known as one of the 'Gaiety Girls', her first London appearance was at the Gaiety theatre in 1894 in *The Shop Girl*. She had many London triumphs, especially *Floradora*, *San Toy*, *The Medal and the Maid*, *Kitty Grey* (her favourite part) and *Butterflies*.

Ada Reeve toured the world indefatigably, making at least eight trips to Australia and almost as many to South Africa, and three to America. She played in vaudeville, panto, musical comedy and straight plays.

During the First World War she entertained the troops in Egypt, India and Australia; while in Australia she raised £100 000 to keep in operation the London club and the Anzac Buffet for overseas soldiers in London – they called her 'Anzac Ada'. This grand old girl continued acting in plays and appearing in vaudeville throughout the 'thirties and 'forties, and in the 'fifties was still making cameo film appearances and broadcasts, and playing the odd role in the theatre. She published her amusing and informative autobiography *Take It for a Fact* in 1954.

49c   GABRIELLE RAY (b. 1883; d. 1973)
               Publisher: Philco Co., London
               Photograph: Johnston & Hoffmann   Hand-coloured
               Postmark: 12 July 1905

Probably more famous as a postcard beauty than as an actress and dancer, 'Gaiety Girl' Gabrielle Ray's career was by no means negligible, and if she was not always the star, her presence was strongly felt. In 1893 she first appeared at the Princess Theatre in *Miami*, and then in various plays and pantomimes. She played Thisbe in *The Orchid* at the Gaiety in 1903, *Lady Madcap* in 1905 at the Prince of Wales, and Lady Dorothy in *The Girl on the Stage* at the Prince of Wales. In 1907 she appeared as Frou-Frou in the first English *Merry Widow*, and in 1911 played Daisy in *The Dollar Princess* at the Gaiety. After absenting herself from the stage for four years, she returned in *Betty* at Daly's in 1915. In 1919-20 she played in variety and in various pantomimes.

49d   CAMILLE CLIFFORD (b. Antwerp, circa 1885; d. ?)
               Publisher: Philco, London
               Photograph: Johnston & Hoffmann   Hand-coloured

A short-lived comet in the theatrical world, 'The Gibson Girl' must have suffered inordinately for her more than unusually pulled-in waist – measuring 14 inches! Belgian-born, Camille Clifford went to America as a girl and there had some minor theatrical experience. Her London début was as Mazie Manhattan in *The Prince of Pilsen* in 1904. Seymour Hicks saw her and gave her the part of Sylvia Gibson in *The Catch of the Season* in the same year; in this role she had a song 'Sylvia, the Gibson Girl'. The Gibson Girl look, inspired by the American artist, Charles Dana Gibson, became the rage in London.

Camille Clifford's next appearance was as the Duchess of Dunmow in *The Belle of Mayfair* in 1906; in this she sang 'Why do they call me a Gibson Girl?', which proved (for no good reason) the hit of the show – much to the chagrin of the leading lady. After a temporary absence from the stage, she reappeared in 1916 in *The Girl of the Future* at the Finsbury Park Empire and went on tour.

PHILCO SERIES 7005 F

a

PHILCO SERIES 7007 C

b

PHILCO SERIES 7006 D

c

PHILCO SERIES 7004 F

d

50a   JEANNE GRANIER (b. 1852; d. 1939)
               Publisher: S.I.P., Paris   Photograph: Reutlinger, Paris
               Hand-coloured

Although Jeanne Granier spent the latter stages of her career as a much-loved actress in Paris, she began as a charming singer in the operettas of Lecocq, the rival of Offenbach. Following in the footsteps of her mother, Irma Granier, who had played the first Nanine in Alexandre Dumas' *La Dame aux Camélias*, she made her début at the Théâtre de la Renaissance (1874) in Offenbach's *La Jolie Parfumeuse*, replacing the ailing star, Louise Théo.

Lecocq heard her and engaged her at once for the first Paris performance of his *Giroflé-Girofla* later that year. She triumphed with her seductive charm, sense of humour and well-schooled voice. Lecocq had her create his next four operettas, all at the Théâtre de la Renaissance: *La Petite Mariée* (1875), *La Marjolaine* (1877), *Le Petit Duc* (1878) and *La Petite Mademoiselle* (1879). The charming *travesti* role in *Le Petit Duc* was her greatest success to date.

It was with Offenbach that she next captivated the public, being considered the true successor to Hortense Schneider. She was splendid as *La Belle Hélène*, Eurydice in *Orphée aux Enfers*, *La Grande Duchesse de Gérolstein*, *La Périchole*, and Boulotte in *Barbe-Bleu*.

50b   MARIETTE SULLY (b. 1874; d. ?)
               Publisher: Reutlinger, Paris   Hand-coloured

Mariette Sully made her début at the Casino de Nice and then sang in Monte Carlo and Bucharest, mainly in secondary roles.

In 1894 she was engaged at the Théâtre des Bouffes-Parisiens, then at the Théâtre des Menus-Plaisirs (*Miss Helyett*) and the Gaîté. At this last theatre she created Audran's *La Poupée* (1896), as well as singing in *Les Cloches de Corneville* and the usual comic operas of the era. In 1898 she created André Messager's *Véronique* at the Théâtre des Folies-Dramatiques, with Jean Périer who became a frequent partner. She also created Messager's *Les Dragons de l'Imperatrice* at the Théâtre des Variétés in 1905.

Popular in Paris and all the major French cities, Mariette Sully was also successful in Lisbon, Madrid and Monte Carlo. She appeared twice in London at Daly's Theatre, in a revival of *Geisha* in 1906, and as Pervenche in the first performance of *Merveilleuses*, a musical adaptation of Sardou which ran for 197 performances in 1906-07.

50c   JULIETTE SIMON-GIRARD (b. 1859; d. 1923)
               Photograph: Reutlinger, Paris, 1901

Juliette Girard, sometimes called Mme Simon-Max, was a very prominent figure in the operettas of her day. She made her début at the Théâtre des Folies-Dramatiques in 1877 in Offenbach's *La Foire de St Laurent*. In the same year she created the role of Serpolette in Planquette's enduring *Les Cloches de Corneville*, and in the following year at the Théâtre des Folies-Dramatiques she played in *Madame Favart* and *La Fille du Tambour-Major* (1879), both important late works of Offenbach.

Her husband, the tenor Simon-Max, sang with her in all these creations as well as in Lecocq's *La Princesse des Canaries* (1883) and Messager's *La Fauvette du Temple* (1885). She sang Hélène in the big revival of Offenbach's *La Belle Hélène* at the Théâtre des Variétés in 1900, followed by three operettas by Varney: *Mlle Georges* in 1901, *Le Chien du Régiment* in 1903, and *Fanfan la Tulipe* in 1904. Her voice was more mezzo-soprano than true soprano, with much richness and volume that allowed her to project into large auditoriums.

50d   EVE LAVALLIERE (b. Nice, 1872; d. 1929)
               Publisher: S.I.P., Paris   Photograph: Reutlinger, Paris
               Hand-coloured

The popular French comedienne Eve Lavallière began her career in operetta and made a spectacular début in the *travesti* role of Oreste in Offenbach's *La Belle Hélène* at the Théâtre des Variétés in 1890. She also played the Baroness in his *La Vie Parisienne* and Siebel in Hervé's *Petit Faust*. Soon, however, she found her way to the straight theatre where she played mostly in modern comedies for three decades, often in the Théâtre des Variétés and the Théâtre Antoine.

Eve Lavallière appeared twice in London – firstly at the Garrick in two comedies by Alfred Capus, *La Veine* and *Les Deux Ecoles*, in both of which she played opposite Lucien Guitry, and again in 1915 at the Ambassador as Suzanne in Pierre Wolff's *Dieu! Que Les Hommes Sont Bêtes*.

JEANNE GRANIER

a

MARIETTE SULLY

b

SIMON GIRARD

c

LAVALLIÈRE

d

51a   BERTRAM WALLIS (b. 1874; d. 1952) as Grand Duke Sergius
in *The Balkan Princess*
Publisher: Rotary Photographic Series
Photograph: Foulsham & Banfield

Bertram Wallis was one of the true matinee idols of English musical theatre. Beginning his career as an actor with Ben Greet's company in 1892, he joined George Alexander in 1896 at the St James' in secondary roles. He toured leading roles in *A Greek Slave* and *San Toy*, and then appeared in London at Daly's and the Apollo in 1902.

Wallis played musical comedy for four years with Charles Frohman's company in New York. On his return to London he had three big successes at the Prince of Wales theatre, all with Isabel Jay as his leading lady – *The King of Cadonia* (1908), *Dear Little Denmark* (1909) and *The Balkan Princess* (1910).

In 1911-12 he played Lehár's Count of Luxembourg with Lily Elsie at Daly's. A few years later he played Baldassare in *The Maid of the Mountains* (1917-20) with Josie Collins, also at Daly's. With the same lady and at the same theatre he played in *A Southern Maid* (1920); again with Josie Collins, but at the Gaiety, he performed in Oscar Strauss' *The Last Waltz* (1922) and *Peter the Great* (1923).

He followed this with Leo Fall's *Mme Pompadour* at Daly's (1923) and Lehár's *The Blue Mazurka* (1927). He continued in revivals of his favourites as well as in new pieces during the 1930s.

51b   SEYMOUR HICKS (b. 1871; d. 1949) as Valentine Brown in
Quality Street
Publisher: Rotary   Photograph: Ellis & Walery

The actor-manager and author Sir Seymour Hicks had a career spanning over fifty years. As a young man (1889-91) he worked with Mr and Mrs Kendal (see **46b**) both in England and America. He played in London at the Court, Toole's, the Gaiety, the Lyric, the Duke of York's, and the Criterion, making three more tours to America before 1900.

In 1901 he played at the Vaudeville in *Bluebell in Fairyland*, which he wrote; he appeared the following year in Barrie's *Quality Street*, and in 1904 *The Catch of the Season* which ran until 1906.

Seymour Hicks built the Aldwych Theatre, where he played in *The Beauty of Bath* (1906), and the Hicks Theatre, where he played in his own *The Gay Gordons* (1907) and *The Dashing Little Duke* (1909). In each of the six plays mentioned here, he appeared with his wife, the charming Ellaline Terriss.

51c   SYDNEY GRANVILLE (b. circa 1880; d. 1959) in *The Gondoliers*
Publisher: Parslee Pictures   Autographed

Sydney Granville spent most of his life singing Gilbert and Sullivan. He joined the D'Oyly Carte Opera Company in 1907, remaining with the company until 1925 (except for the years of the First World War). He then toured Australia, singing Gilbert and Sullivan.

Again at the D'Oyly Carte fairly constantly from 1929 to 1939, his roles included Giuseppe, later Don Alhambra, in *The Gondoliers*, Samuel and the Sergeant of Police in *The Pirates of Penzance*, Strephon and Private Willis in *Iolanthe*, the Usher and the Judge in *Trial by Jury*, Grosvenor in *Patience*, Pish-Tush and Pooh-Bah in *The Mikado*.

Granville appeared in a film of *The Mikado* in 1938 and retired from the D'Oyly Carte in 1942.

51d   GERTIE MILLAR (b. 1879; d. 1952) and ROBERT EVETT
(b. 1874; d. 1949) as Franzi & Lieutenant Niki in *A Waltz Dream*
Publisher: Rotary   Photograph: Foulsham & Banfield
Postmark: 14 May 1903

Gertie Millar was one of the most beloved performers as well as one of the best on the English stage. She began as a 'Gaiety Girl' and had big hits in *The Orchid* (1903), *The Spring Chicken* (1905), *The New Aladdin* (1906), *The Girls of Gottenburg* (1907), *Our Miss Gibbs* (1909), *The Quaker Girl* (1911), *Gypsy Love* (1912), *The Dancing Mistress* (1912), and *The Marriage Market* (1913). Her first husband was the composer Lionel Monkton, and she finished her days as the Countess of Dudley.

Robert Evett began as a member of the D'Oyly Carte, later performing in such comic operas as *A Princess of Kensington* (1903), *The Earl and the Girl* (1903), *The Little Michus* (1905), *The Merry Widow* (1907), and *The Girl in the Train* (1912). He became the Managing Director of Daly's Theatre and produced *The Maid of the Mountains* (1917-20) and other shows until his retirement in 1925.

A Waltz Dream was first performed in London at the Hicks Theatre on 7 March 1908, with Gertie Millar as Franzi and Robert Evett as Lieutenant Niki. It was conducted by the composer Oscar Strauss.

2387 W ROTARY PHOTO, E.C.   MR. BERTRAM WALLIS   FOULSHAM & BANFIELD
AS "GRAND DUKE SERGIUS" IN "THE BALKAN PRINCESS."

a

4224 A   MR. SEYMOUR HICKS   ROTARY PHOTO, E.C.

b

PUBLISHED BY   MR. SYDNEY GRANVILLE   PARKSLEE PICTURES
No. 92   AS "GIUSEPPE" IN "THE GONDOLIERS"
(D'OYLY CARTE OPERA CO.)

c

4952 R ROTARY PHOTO, E.C.   FOULSHAM & BANFIELD.
MISS GERTIE MILLAR   MR. ROBERT EVETT
AS "FRANZI"   AS "LIEUT. NIKI."
IN "A WALTZ DREAM."

d

Theatres   **52a**   LONDON HIPPODROME

The London Hippodrome opened on 15 January 1900 with circus and variety acts. Situated on the corner of Cranbourne Street and Charing Cross Road, it was originally intended as a rather spectacular music-hall. It had a capacity of 1340 seats.

Many celebrated performers appeared there, including Lillie Langtry, Réjane, Cinquevalli, Loïe Fuller, Zena Dare, Harry Fragson, Cicely Courtneidge, Yvette Guilbert, Ada Reeve, George Robey, Sophie Tucker and Leoncavallo.

Some reconstruction was carried out in 1909 and the circus area was replaced by stalls. There were ballet concerts, with Ludmilla Schollar, at the London Hippodrome in 1909 and 1910, and the first performance of *Swan Lake* in England was given there with Olga Preobrajenska in 1910.

Many musical comedies were played there, including Ivor Novello's *Perchance to Dream* which ran for 1022 performances. It was turned into a restaurant-cabaret in 1958, and re-opened as The Talk of the Town, Hippodrome Corner.

52b   THE OPERA HOUSE, BUXTON
                     Publisher: F. Wright, Stationer, Buxton

This handsome Edwardian theatre situated in the Derbyshire spa town of Buxton was designed by the famous theatre architect, Frank Matcham. It opened in 1903 with the play *Mrs Willoughby's Kiss*, starring Florence St John, and for two decades housed vaudeville, pantomime, burlesque, circus, boxing revues, plays, opera, ballet and musical comedy. West End successes were brought to Buxton by leading theatrical, operatic and ballet companies of the day, including those of F. R. Benson, Beerbohm Tree, Martin Harvey, Lena Ashwell, Carl Rosa, D'Oyly Carte and Anna Pavlova; famous personalities who appeared there included Mrs Patrick Campbell, Marie Lloyd, Gertrude Lawrence, Evelyn Laye, Gracie Fields, Hermione Gingold and Robert Newton.

Silent films were first shown in the Opera House in 1913 and 'talkies' from 1932. After the First World War fewer professional companies visited Buxton and the theatre was used principally as a cinema and for Christmas pantomimes, with the exception of a festival of plays, opera and ballet given by the Old Vic and Sadler's Wells companies that ran for six seasons between 1937 and 1942. In 1979 the theatre, closed for some years, was meticulously restored to its original design, gaining a much enlarged orchestra pit. It re-opened in July 1979 with *Lucia di Lammermoor* and is now host to various regional theatre and opera companies, and to the annual Buxton International Festival.

52c   L'OPERA, PARIS
                     Publisher: P.G.H. & Co., London   Signed: Loir Luigi

Officially known as the Académie Nationale de Musique, Théâtre National de L'Opéra, this beautifully ornate and luxurious theatre in the Place de L'Opéra was designed by Charles Garnier, and opened in 1875. The opening programme on 5 January contained the first two acts of Halévy's *La Juive*, the Scene of the Blessing of the Swords from *Les Huguenots*, and the first tableau from Act II of *La Source* with music by Delibes. On 8 January the first complete opera, *La Juive*, was performed.

This building replaces the one in the Rue Peletier where so many of the greatest works in French nineteenth-century theatre were created and which housed the greatest singers and dancers in the world.

a

The Opera House, Buxton.   F. Wright, Stationer, Buxton.

b

l'Opéra.

c

PUBLICATIONS

FRANCE:
Neudin, L'Argus International des Cartes Postales
Les Editions de l'Amateur
6 Rue Milton
75009, Paris

Le Premier Annuaire Mondial
An annual publication which lists books, the address of numerous shops and publications
throughout the world.

UNITED KINGDOM
Antiques Trade Gazette
17 Whitcomb Street
London, WC2H 7PL
A weekly paper which lists all UK fairs and auctions, as well as many in other countries, and
includes sales reports, classified ads, etc.

Picture Postcard Monthly
15 Debdale Lane
Keyworth
Nottingham, NG12 5HT
'The top magazine for postcard collectors worldwide'; includes news and articles, diaries of
events, classified ads, etc.

International Postcard Market (IPM) Promotions
2 Frederick Gardens
Brighton, BN1 4TB
'Europe's leading dealers in picture postcards'; publishers of regular, combined magazine/sales
catalogue, as well as books on picture postcards.

RF Postcards
17 Hilary Crescent
Rayleigh, Essex
'One of UK's largest dealers and organizers of regular Postcard Fairs'; publish yearly catalogue.

Picton's Priced Postcard Catalogue and Handbook
BPH Publications Ltd
Citadel Works
Bath Road, Chippenham
Wiltshire, SN15 2AA
An updated price guide; historical information; useful addresses.

AUCTION HOUSES
(UNITED KINGDOM)

The principal auction houses which sell postcards in the UK are:

Neales of Nottingham
192 Mansfield Road
Nottingham, NG1 3HX

SPA (Specialised Postcard Auctions)
12 Suffolk Road
Cheltenham
Gloucestershire, GL50 2AQ

Garnet Langton Auctions
Burlington Arcade
Bournemouth, Dorset

Bonhams
Montpelier Galleries
Montpelier Street
London, SW7 1HH

Christie's South Kensington
85 Old Brompton Road
London, SW7 3LD

Phillips
7 Blenheim Street
London, W1Y OAS

Index